Life Coaching

D1312937

The way we think profoundly influences the way we feel. Therefore, it can be said that learning to think differently can enable us to feel and act differently. Derived from the methods of cognitive behaviour therapy, this book shows you how to tackle self-defeating thinking and replace it with a problem-solving outlook.

This book gives clear and helpful advice on:

- Dealing with troublesome emotions
- Overcoming procrastination
- Becoming assertive
- Tackling poor time management
- Persisting at problem-solving
- Handling criticism constructively
- Taking risks and making better decisions.

The second edition of this book, which has been revised and updated with a new chapter on developing resilience, will be invaluable to all those who are interested in becoming more personally effective in their everyday lives, and to counsellors, coaches and psychologists, students and qualified alike.

Michael Neenan is Associate Director of the Centre for Stress Management and Centre for Coaching, Blackheath, and a BABCP accredited cognitive behavioural therapist. He has written and edited over 20 books.

Windy Dryden is Professor of Psychotherapeutic Studies at Goldsmiths College, University of London and is an international authority on rational emotive behaviour therapy (REBT). He has worked in psychotherapy for over 30 years and is the author and editor of over 195 books.

Life Coaching

A cognitive behavioural approach
Second edition

Michael Neenan and
Windy Dryden

Routledge
Taylor & Francis Group

LONDON AND NEW YORK

First published 2014
by Routledge
27 Church Road, Hove, East Sussex BN3 2FA

Simultaneously published in the USA and Canada
by Routledge
711 Third Avenue, New York, NY 10017

Routledge is an imprint of the Taylor & Francis Group, an informa business

British Library Cataloguing in Publication Data
A catalogue record for this book is available from the British Library
Library of Congress Cataloging in Publication Data
Neenan, Michael.
    Life coaching : a cognitive behavioural approach / Michael Neenan and
    Windy Dryden.—Second edition.
    pages cm
    Includes bibliographical references and index.
    1. Conduct of life. 2. Cognitive therapy. I. Dryden, Windy. II. Title.
    BF637.C5N44 2013
    158.1—dc23
    2013001781

ISBN: 978-0-415-66182-9 (hbk)
ISBN: 978-0-415-66183-6 (pbk)
ISBN: 978-0-203-75831-1 (ebk)

Typeset in Times New Roman
by Swales & Willis Ltd, Exeter, Devon

To my son, Laurence, who remains a
constant source of inspiration to me.
M. N.

Contents

Preface

The way you think about events in your life profoundly influences the way you feel about them; change the way you think and this will, in turn, change the way you feel. This is the essence of a widely practised and research-based counselling approach called cognitive behaviour therapy (CBT). Understanding your view of events provides the insight into why you feel and act in the ways that you do (for example, you're anxious about public speaking and avoid it because you fear that your performance will be less than perfect). Armed with this knowledge, you can then decide if you want to change this viewpoint in favour of one that is more likely to bring you better results in life (for example, 'Competence and confidence will come through actually doing it. Doing it as well as I can is far more important than doing it perfectly'). How this is achieved is the subject of this book. It's important to point out, in order to correct misconceptions, that CBT does not advocate positive thinking. The main problem with positive thinking is described by Burkeman (2012: 16):

> A person who has resolved to 'think positive' must constantly scan his or her mind for negative thoughts – there's no other way that the mind could ever gauge its success at the operation – yet that scanning will draw attention to the presence of negative thoughts. (Worse, if the negative thoughts start to predominate, a vicious spiral may kick in, since the failure to think positively may become the trigger for a new stream of self-berating thoughts, about not thinking positively enough).

CBT helps clients to develop realistic, balanced and flexible appraisals of events (positive thinking is none of these things and we encourage our clients not to be afraid of, obsess about or berate themselves for having negative thoughts). CBT is not interested in negative thinking per se, but targets those negative, distorted thoughts and beliefs most closely connected to your emotional upsets and unproductive behaviours. As you will see, changing your thinking is easy to say but harder to do.

Several decades of research evidence has demonstrated the effectiveness of CBT and it's recommended by the National Institute for Health and Clinical Excellence (NICE) as the first line treatment in the NHS for treating a wide range of psychological disorders (NICE, 2005). Adapting CBT to coaching has also meant developing an evidence base to support its use in, for example, the workplace (Neenan and Palmer, 2012). So, what is the difference between CBT and cognitive behavioural coaching (CBC)? The major difference is that CBT sees people with diagnosed mental health problems such as major depression, post-traumatic stress disorder and panic disorder, whereas CBC focuses on personal and professional development, for example, helping a person to manage the new responsibilities that come with promotion. Does this mean that clients who come for coaching have no problems to deal with? Certainly not. For example, over the years we have seen plenty of business executives who have some of the following difficulties: performance anxiety, procrastination, perfectionism, fears of failure, worried about being seen as weak or not in control, poor time management, having a short fuse when under pressure or things go wrong ... the list goes on. To complicate matters further, some clients want coaching when they really require counselling and we hope the coach is shrewd enough to know the difference between the two approaches (Buckley and Buckley, 2006).

What these two approaches do have in common is helping clients to remove their psychological blocks to goal achievement, for example, being able to travel on the Underground without fear (CBT) or not being overly anxious when making a presentation to the management board (CBC). With this commonality in mind, our definition of CBC is helping individuals to develop their capabilities in a chosen area, or areas, with a particular focus on the beliefs, emotions and behaviours that help or hinder this development. We believe that CBC is ideally suited to this purpose.

CBC does not offer any quick fixes to achieve personal change or 'magic away' your difficulties; it does emphasise that sustained effort and commitment are required for a successful outcome to your life challenges or difficulties. So if you're the kind of person who wants great change for little effort, then this book is not for you! Remember, it's not just reading a self-help book that changes you but the amount of hard work you expend on putting into daily practice what the book recommends.

Who is this book for? Well, it's aimed at that neglected species in this dumbing-down age, the intelligent reader. This person keeps her critical faculties sharp by engaging with new ideas, welcomes opposing viewpoints, is unafraid to change her mind and seeks opportunities for self-development. Even these fine qualities, however, cannot prevent you from underperforming or becoming stuck in certain areas of your life.

In this book, we look at some common difficulties and how to tackle them such as procrastination, unassertiveness, poor time management, not dealing constructively with criticism and lacking persistence in the pursuit of your goals. We hope that within these eleven chapters you will find some attitudes to adopt and skills to acquire that will keep you in good stead throughout your life and thereby help you to deal with whatever comes your way; in other words, self-coaching to cope with life's vicissitudes. While we would obviously urge you to read the whole book in order to get its full benefit, each chapter is self-contained so you can cherry-pick your way through the book if you wish. The clients in this book are composite characters in order to protect their identity and the dialogue excerpts are not verbatim but reconstructed for the sake of clarity in order to emphasise certain points and avoid the verbal clutter (such as going off at tangents, rambling) that often occurs in actual coaching sessions.

A final word: in the eleven years between the first and second editions of this book, coaching passed the fad phase of its existence and is now experiencing its boom years: growing media interest; increasing use of coaching for personal, professional and organisational growth; and the rush of people wanting to train as coaches (some joke that there are more coaches than there are clients!). It looks like coaching has become a permanent resource for personal and professional development.

Acknowledgements

We wish to thank *Counselling*, the Journal of the British Association for Counselling, for permission to reprint material contained in Chapters 3 and 7.

Chapter 1

Dealing with troublesome emotions

Introduction

Samantha enjoyed her job as a sales rep and had worked for the same company for five years. Despite her considerable experience in the job, she still felt intense bouts of anxiety when giving presentations or meeting new and important customers: 'This should not be happening to me after five years in the job.'

Raymond liked to see himself as calm and cool under pressure, a man who took problems in his stride, but his behaviour did not always reflect his self-image – he often flew into a rage if, for example, he could not find his car keys, or assembling DIY furniture proved too complicated: 'Why do I behave like that? Why can't I control myself?'

Janet had to get a full-time job to make ends meet and therefore had to find a childminder for her two children. Even though she knew they were being well looked after, she still felt guilty about 'abandoning' them: 'I should be there to pick them up from school and give them their tea.'

Brian could be clumsy sometimes and felt hurt when some of his friends laughed at him for tripping over his own feet or bumping into things: 'It's not fair when they laugh at me. I can't help being uncoordinated.'

In each of these four cases, the emotions prove troublesome because though not incapacitating or requiring professional attention, they nevertheless hover in the background, unresolved and ready to intrude again.

When I (MN) asked each person what caused their troublesome emotions, they said, respectively, giving presentations and meeting important customers, searching for car keys and doing DIY, having to go to work and leaving the children with someone else, and being laughed at for acting clumsily. In other words, external events or others create their feelings. While this view of emotional causation is a popular one – count how many times in the next week you or a friend says something like 'He/she/it makes me feel this way' – this doesn't make it an accurate one. The most important part in the chain of emotional causation has been left out – yourself! In order to experience an emotional reaction to an event, you first have to evaluate the personal significance of the event. An American psychologist, the late Dr Albert Ellis (1994), used a simple model to show how we largely upset ourselves about negative events in our lives:

A – activating event: the end of a relationship
B – beliefs or thoughts: 'Without her, I'm worthless.'
C – emotional and behavioural consequences: depression and withdrawal
   from social activity

You may say that A caused C ('Who wouldn't be depressed if their partner left them?') and in CBT language this is called A–C thinking (events cause our emotions). This viewpoint overlooks individual variations to the same event, that is, not everyone would feel depressed about the end of a relationship: one person is anxious about coping alone, another is angry at being dumped, a third person is relieved that it's over while a fourth feels ashamed that he did not fight harder to preserve the relationship. Therefore, in order to understand C you need to focus on B, not A; this is called B–C thinking (our beliefs mainly determine our emotions). You may get angry at this point (what are you telling yourself?) because you think we are minimising or paying no attention to bad events in people's lives. Not so. Events at A can contribute powerfully to your emotional problems but your beliefs and thoughts at B ultimately determine how you feel at C. We will use an extreme example to illustrate this point. Viktor Frankl, an eminent psychiatrist who died in 1997, was spared the gas chambers at Auschwitz and put to work in the camp, enduring hideous suffering but never losing hope. He famously observed that 'everything can be taken from a man but one thing: the last of the human freedoms – to choose one's attitude in any given circumstances, to choose one's own way' (1985: 86). Choosing an attitude to cope with adversity is your responsibility and no one else's.

Whatever the situation, you can choose how you wish to react to it because you do have some measure of free will. Events, whether past or present, do not impose their feelings on you; your feelings are largely determined by your current attitudes to these events. In other words: *you feel as you think* (Burns, 1981).

Ants in your mind

When you're feeling bad (for example, angry), ask yourself: 'What is going through my mind at this moment?' in order to tune into what are called automatic negative thoughts, or ANTs (Beck, 1976). These thoughts are called automatic because they pop into your mind involuntarily and therefore are not the product of reflection or reasoning, seem plausible at the time of their occurrence and are difficult to 'turn off' (ANTs can also be images, daydreams and fantasies). Two examples:

1. Your partner is late coming home and you feel anxious because your mind is flooded with disturbing thoughts (for example, 'What if he's been involved in a pile-up or hit by a drunk driver?') and images (such as imagining him trapped in the burning wreckage). He eventually arrives home safe and you now feel relieved because you are able to 'turn off' the anxiety-provoking thoughts and images by telling yourself, 'There was nothing to worry about after all. I was just being really silly.'

2. You see your wife in the high street talking to and embracing another man and immediately feel jealous: 'Who the hell is that? Why are they laughing so much? They're having an affair. She's planning to leave me.' When she gets home, you interrogate her and discover it's her brother who she hasn't seen for several years. You now feel ashamed because you are thinking: 'I'm so stupid for jumping to conclusions. I've shown my wife how jealous and insecure I am.'

In order to change the way you feel, you need to change the way you think; added to the ABC model are D and E. D is for disputing or questioning your upsetting thinking (D can also stand for discussion as some coaches can get carried away by taking an adversarial stance towards their clients, as implied by the term disputing). When you're emotionally upset your thinking usually becomes closed and rigid; questions that encourage rational reflection help your thinking to recover its openness and flexibility, for example, 'What's the evidence in my life to conclude that I'm worthless?'; 'How will believing I'm worthless help me to find another relationship?' 'Would I call my daughter worthless if her relationship ended?' Disputing employs the technique of decentring whereby you stand back from your upsetting thinking and examine it in an objective way.

We would suggest that a lot of your emotional difficulties are largely self-defined, that is, you define them in a way that leads to emotional trouble. For example, you imagine that making a mistake in front of others would be a disaster instead of a setback (anxiety); smacking your child means you're a wicked mother (guilt) rather than a mother who had a momentary loss of control; if others discover you're dyslexic, then this would expose you as an idiot (shame) instead of someone who has difficulties with reading and spelling. Through disputing or thinking about your thinking in more helpful ways by using reason and logic, you can learn to develop an effective (E) outlook that promotes greater emotional and behavioural stability in your life.

When you're questioning your thinking, you're acting as a personal scientist, treating your ideas and beliefs as hypotheses (assumptions) rather than as facts and reality-testing them in order to find alternative explanations and behaviours that are more helpful in solving your emotional problems. Typical questions to ask yourself in order to challenge your ANTs include:

- Is the thought true? If it is, what is the worst that can happen and could I cope with it?
- Which distortions are present in my thinking? (these distortions can be found at surface and deeper levels of thought; see core beliefs below)
- If my friend had the same problem as me, would I judge her as harshly as I judge myself? If the answer is no, then what makes me so different? What advice would I offer her that I am not prepared to follow myself?
- What is the evidence for and against this thought?
- How might things look in three or six months' time?
- What would happen if I entered that situation instead of continually avoiding it?

Distorted thinking

When we're upset, we often process incoming information in a consistently biased and distorted way that maintains our low mood, angry behaviour or anxious state. Some of the common distortions (also known as thinking traps) found in emotional problems include:

- All-or-nothing thinking: seeing events in extreme terms that allows for no shades of grey or middle ground, for example, 'If I can't have her, then no one else will do.' The antidote to this kind of thinking is balanced, non-extreme appraisals of a situation that allow you more options to choose from, such as, 'She would have been the ideal partner but I'm sure that I can be happy with other women.'
- Magnification/minimisation: exaggerating the negative and reducing the positive, for example, 'I stumbled over a sentence and turned

the talk into a disaster' and 'Some people said they enjoyed the talk but what do they know?' What is required from you in tackling these distortions is a sense of proportion, such as thinking 'Stumbling over a sentence was just a hiccup and the rest of the talk proceeded smoothly' and 'Some people enjoyed the talk which indicates that it went reasonably well.'

* Personalisation: taking too much blame for events you're not to- tally responsible for, like, 'I made my wife have an affair.' With this distortion, it's important to distinguish between your actual and presumed responsibility for an event – you may have contributed to marital discord by working long hours at the office but your wife chose to have an affair to satisfy her needs.

* Emotional reasoning: you believe something is true because you feel it so strongly. For example, 'I feel like a failure, so I must be one.' While feelings are important, they're not facts or reflect objective reality; so it's important to examine evidence dispassionately in or- der to arrive at an accurate assessment of the situation, with thoughts such as 'It's true that I've had some recent failures but they don't make me a failure as a person. The part does not define the whole.' As Gilbert observes: 'When we use feelings to do the work of our rational minds, we are liable to get into trouble' (1997: 93).

* Mind-reading: the ability to know the thoughts of others without using the normal means of communication, for example, 'My boss doesn't say so, but I know he thinks I'm an idiot.' Often, negative thoughts such as these are in your mind and therefore you imagine they must also be in the minds of others. Instead of mind-reading, ask the other person or wait until you have firm evidence to sup- port your beliefs. If you did ask your boss and he denied thinking you were an idiot and you didn't believe him, you've gone back to mind-reading!

* Labelling: you attach a global and negative label to yourself based on specific behaviours, for example, 'I failed to pass the exam, so that makes me a moron.' Here you're assuming your behaviour reflects your totality as a complex and fallible (imperfect) human being. As Leahy succinctly asks: 'Is it a behavior that fails or the entire person?' (1996: 99). If you want to use labels, then attach them to your behaviour instead of yourself, for example, 'I failed the exam but that certainly doesn't make me a moron.' Focusing on behaviour change ('What can I do to help me pass the exam at the second attempt?') is more constructive than experiencing the consequences of self-condemnation ('As I'm a moron, there's no

point whatsoever in attempting the exam again and bringing more disgrace on myself').

- Discounting the positive: any positive experiences or qualities are disregarded, for example, 'People say the workshop was a success but they are just trying to make me feel better because they know it was a failure.' Discounting the positive will make your life seem relentlessly one-sided and maintain your low mood. Including the positive as well as the negative will lead to a more balanced assessment of your present difficulties (for example, 'Certainly the workshop had its flaws, but I very much doubt that these people are all banding together to lie to me').

- Shoulds and musts: these are usually in the form of rigid rules of living that you impose on yourself, others and/or life, for example, 'I must never show any weaknesses'; 'You should always give me what I want'; 'I must not have too much pressure in my life.' When these rules are not obeyed, you will often condemn yourself (thinking, for example, 'I'm spineless'), others ('You bastard') or life ('I hate this stinking world'). Rigid musts and shoulds make you subservient to a totalitarian system of thinking. The alternative to rigid rules are flexible ones which allow you to acknowledge and act in accordance with the reality that yourself, others and/or the world rarely fit with how things must or should be.

- Mental filter: focusing exclusively on one negative aspect of a situation and thereby judging the whole situation by it, for example, 'I knocked over a glass of wine and the whole evening was a disaster because of it.' Burns memorably likens mental filtering to 'the drop of ink that discolors the entire beaker of water' (1981: 40). Instead of dwelling on one aspect of the situation, stand back and view the whole situation in an objective way, for example, 'Spilling the wine did lead to some embarrassment on my part and some irritation on theirs, but once that was over, we all seemed to have had a pretty good time.'

- Fortune-telling: believing you can predict the future in a consistently accurate way. While you probably do make some accurate predictions such as 'This new job is going to entail a lot of hard work and responsibility' others will be wide of the mark, particularly when you're in a pessimistic or negative frame of mind, for example, 'I failed my driving test. I'll never be able to pass it.' You may consider that your predictions are accurate because you act in ways that make them come true. Say you predict that you will be unable to give up smoking, and when you try to quit, you start feeling irritable and moody – instead of tolerating these feelings as part of the withdrawal symptoms, you conclude that you cannot cope with them and resume smoking. One way to assess how good a fortune-teller you are is to write down some of your predictions and review them objectively in a few months' time to determine how accurate they are.

- Overgeneralisation: drawing sweeping conclusions based on a single event or insufficient information, for example, 'Because my relationship has ended, I'll never find anyone else and I will always be unhappy.' Overgeneralisation can be brought under control by examining what evidence you have for your sweeping conclusions and advancing alternative arguments in the light of this review, such as 'My relationship has ended and it will be hard to find another partner if all I do is mope about at home, but I'm more likely to find someone else and have some happiness if I start to socialise again.'

- Catastrophising: always assuming the worst and, if it occurs, your inability to cope with it, for example, 'I'm sure my boyfriend is going to dump me because he doesn't phone me as much as he used to. If he dumps me, I'll completely fall apart and never get over the rejection.' McKay, Davis and Fanning state that 'there are no limits to an active catastrophic imagination' (2011: 30). Challenging catastrophising involves, among other things, asking what is the probable outcome versus the possible outcome? In the above example, the probable outcome might be that the person is not going to be dumped, but nonetheless, the relationship is going through a difficult period. On the other hand, the possible outcome might be rejection and therefore the person needs to learn how to adapt constructively to this grim reality in order to tolerate rejection and not fall apart (decatastrophising). It's important that you learn to play the odds more accurately: how many of your catastrophic predictions have actually occurred? (possible answer: 'One, but it wasn't as bad as I thought'). Next time you catastrophise, remember the odds, that is, remember that it's highly unlikely that the dreaded outcome will occur.

Core beliefs

The distortions in thinking outlined in the previous section frequently stem from underlying negative core beliefs which are usually formed much earlier in your life (but can be newly formed if, for example, you currently condemn yourself as weak for not recovering quickly enough from a serious car accident) and are activated from their dormant state when you're upset – we like to see these core beliefs as 'light sleepers'. Technically speaking, this activation occurs when the situation matches the content of your core beliefs: so if I (MN) believe it's terrible not to be loved, I will probably get depressed if my partner says she never really loved me and then leaves. This matching process has been likened to a key fitting into a lock in order to open the door to emotional upset.

Core beliefs are global and absolute (for example, 'I'm incompetent'; 'Nobody can be trusted'; 'The world is against me'). Once active, these beliefs pass into your awareness and determine how you will view a situation. For example, you're passed over for promotion and make yourself depressed because you believe 'I'm not good enough' and you now question whether there is anything good in your life. Once the emotional crisis has passed, the belief returns to its dormant state but ready to be reactivated at a later date unless this belief is modified or changed in some way. Negative core beliefs leave you vulnerable to future episodes of emotional upset. To uncover core beliefs, you can use a method known as the downward arrow technique which follows the personal implications of a 'hot' (that is, emotionally charged) automatic negative thought by asking for the meaning of each thought revealed (Burns, 1981). For example, Jane was anxious about attending a party because she thought:

- 'I won't get off with anyone'
    - If that's true, what will that mean to me?
- 'That I'll go home alone'
    - If that's true, what will that mean to me?
- 'No one fancies me'
    - If that's true, what will that mean to me?
- 'If no one fancies me, then I'll be all alone' (underlying assumption)
    - If that's true, what will that mean about me?
- 'That I'm undesirable' (core belief)

Asking yourself what a thought means *to* you often reveals an underlying assumption which is identified by an 'if . . . then' construction; asking what it means *about* you usually reveals a core belief (Beck, 2011). When you're using the downward arrow technique, assume temporarily that each thought is true in order to concentrate your mind on revealing a core belief. If you disrupt this technique by challenging each thought (for example, 'Do I always go home alone?') you will probably prevent yourself from reaching the core belief.

Once a core belief is revealed, you can ask yourself the same questions and identify the distortions in your thinking as described above, for example, 'How does not getting off with someone at a party mean I'm undesirable?'; 'I'm using labelling and all-or-nothing thinking.' If Jane wants to change her view of herself as undesirable, then how would she like to see herself? She said 'desirable' but this self-image was a balanced one, that is, it incorporated 'getting off with someone' as well as rejection and indifference to her. Her concept of desirability was a flexible one and able to provide more emotional resilience in times of being alone whereas her concept of undesirability was an inflexible one leading to prolonged bouts of unhappiness.

To reinforce her new self-image, Jane went through her life to find historical evidence to support it (such as boyfriends, marriage, affairs) and kept a diary for several months to collect current evidence (for example being chatted up, a few dates, hearing that 'someone fancies me'). Jane also conducted an analysis of the development of her 'undesirability' self-image ('I always thought that if someone I fancied didn't fancy me then I was undesirable. I realise now how simplistic that was') in order to understand the adverse effects this belief has had on her life and functioning. When Jane's new self-image 'collapsed' or was 'shaken' from time to time, this usually meant that she had reverted temporarily to believing she was undesirable (because, for example, someone she fancied did not reciprocate) and started examining the evidence again to reject this conclusion. In this way, the ideas underpinning her old self-image were gradually weakened while the ideas supporting her new self-image were gradually strengthened.

Some common troublesome emotions

In this section, as well as describing the main features of these emotions, we also provide some techniques for tackling them.

Anxiety

Anxiety is based on future-orientated thinking that encompasses themes of danger or threat where you will be vulnerable in some way. People frequently overestimate the dangerousness of a given situation and underestimate their ability to cope with it. The threat or danger can be viewed along a continuum of time from imminent ('Oh my God! I'm going to pass out'), to the near future (for example, 'I know I'll show myself up when I meet my husband's friends this weekend') and longer term (for example, 'I'm sure this lump on my shoulder is going to prove cancerous in a couple of years' time'). When you're anxious you may experience some of the following symptoms: breathlessness, palpitations, trembling, sweating, dizziness, hot flushes or 'jelly legs'. These symptoms are the same for a physical danger (such as a burglar in your house) as for a psychosocial threat (such as fear of rejection). Depending on your evaluation of the situation you might strike out (fight), escape the situation (flight), become immobilized (freeze) or collapse (faint).

Fear can be distinguished from anxiety: the former is a perceived threat to your safety or security (for example, 'I know I'm going to freeze in front of all those people when I start my presentation and look a complete idiot') and the latter is a more prolonged feeling of unease usually triggered by the initial evaluation of threat (Clark and Beck, 2012) such as feeling on edge before, during and after the presentation. When you feel anxious you may try to avoid or withdraw from the threatening situation or seek reassurance from others that the feared outcome will not occur. This behavioural strategy provides short-term relief from anxiety but reinforces it in the longer term. When you're anxious you will often engage in 'What if . . .?' thinking (for example, 'What if I lose control?' 'What if she doesn't like me?' 'What if the plane crashes?') which usually ends in some imagined catastrophe (for example, 'I'll lose control of myself in public and people will laugh at me. I'll never recover from the humiliation of it'). 'What if . . .?' anxious thinking can be transformed into 'then what . . .?' problem-solving thinking (Padesky and Greenberger, 1995). For example:

What if I can't answer the question?	Then admit I can't. Ask the audience if someone can, or say I will find out the answer.
What if they think I'm stupid?	Then I am probably jumping to conclusions as usual; even if some of them think that, I don't have to agree with them!
What if I do agree that I'm stupid?	Then I am being very harsh on myself. Being unable to answer a question is simply that. I don't have to turn it into a stick to beat myself with. Learn to focus on improving my performance, not putting myself down.
What if I can't learn to do that?	Then that would be unfortunate, but it's highly likely I will be able to learn it if I put it into daily practice so it becomes a lifelong habit.

Another challenge to 'What if . . .?' negative thinking is to ask 'What if . . .?' positive questions, such as, 'What if I keep control of myself?'; 'What if she does like me?'; 'What if the plane doesn't crash?' As Newman observes:

> When you are anxious you rarely if ever give equal time to the positive, literally *opposite* question, 'What if I succeed?' Therein lies a fundamental cognitive bias, because an objective assessment of future outcomes requires the careful consideration of both the positive and negative possibilities.
>
> (2000:140; emphasis in original)

The obvious way to deal with anxiety is to face your fears. This can involve working through a hierarchy of fears (that is, from least to most frightening) at a pace that is challenging for you, but not overwhelming. It's important to remain in each feared situation until your anxiety has subsided through cognitive change, for example, 'It used to be absolutely awful being in the same room as a spider but now it's just unpleasant.' Leaving the situation before your anxiety has significantly reduced is likely to reinforce your beliefs that you're in immediate danger and your anxiety is intolerable. We would suggest that it's our statements that often create our anxiety such as 'I can't stand it' and 'It would be awful if that happened'. What does it mean when you say 'I can't stand it'? Your imminent death, psychological meltdown or permanent misery? The 'it' usually refers to the considerable discomfort you will experience when you tackle your fears instead of your usual practice of avoiding them. You can choose to 'stand it' and redefine awful as unpleasant or uncomfortable as part of your decatastrophising outlook which will help to achieve your longer-term goals of overcoming your fears.

Finally, don't wait until you feel comfortable, courageous or confident before you tackle your fears otherwise you'll probably be waiting a long time. You can deal with your anxiety while feeling anxious. Doing what you're afraid of eventually extinguishes the fear and allows you to focus on other, more enjoyable activities.

Depression

Depression can range from mild to severe and involves the theme of loss (of a partner, job, self-esteem, religious faith, sexual potency). Self-devaluation frequently follows a loss (for example, 'Because I'm impotent, I'm no longer a real man'). When people are depressed they usually withdraw from activities that were previously enjoyable and into themselves, thus reinforcing their depressed state. The negative content of a depressed person's thinking has been called the cognitive triad of depression (Beck *et al.*, 1979): you have a negative view of yourself ('I'm no good'), the world (for example, 'Everything is against me') and your future (for example, 'I'll never get over this depression').

Accompanying this bleak outlook are, inter alia, loss of pleasure, interest, libido, appetite and motivation, poor sleep pattern, rumination, indecisiveness, and suicidal thoughts. Hauck (1974) identifies three causes of depression:

1. Self-blame: continually criticising or despising yourself for your failures and setbacks in life (for example, 'My marriage failed. I can't do anything right. I'm totally useless'). Hauck points out that 'it makes practically no difference what you blame yourself for, just so long as you give yourself hell for it' (1974: 8–9). If you keep on blaming yourself, how will that help you to correct your faults and improve your behaviour?
2. Self-pity: feeling sorry for yourself over the misfortunes in your life (for example, 'I didn't deserve to lose my job. Why me? What's the world got against me?'). Life is often arbitrary and unfair but you forget this point when you believe that you deserve to be treated differently, that you have been marked out as a 'special case'.
3. Other-pity: feeling sorry for the woes of others (for example, 'It's terrible that famine kills so many children'). Getting depressed over the misfortunes of others does nothing to help them in a practical sense, so what useful purpose does your depression serve? Does your pain lessen the suffering of others?

Such bleak thinking is characteristic of depression but, you might argue, surely there are some events, like the death of a partner, that justify being depressed; therefore, in these circumstances, one's thinking is not distorted. Having lost a loved partner is distressing but the distortions might creep into your thinking because, for example, you believe 'I'll never be happy again' or 'Now that he's gone, all I can look forward to is loneliness'. You're predicting your future based on how you're feeling and thinking at the present time, but you cannot accurately know how your future will turn out (that can only be determined by looking back, not forward). You can choose to find another partner and see if there is happiness still to be had. Burns distinguishes between sadness and depression: 'Sadness is a normal emotion created by realistic perceptions that describe a negative event involving loss in an undistorted way. Depression is an illness that *always* results from thoughts that are distorted in some way' (1981: 207; emphasis in original).

Lazarus (1999) suggests that the mood in sadness is not despairing because you've accepted that the loss (such as the death of a partner) is irrevocable, that is, it cannot be restored. Once accepted, you're able to get on with your life. Depression is also tackled by developing a daily activity schedule to keep you busy – action forces you to interrupt your depression-inducing thinking. You probably will not feel motivated to undertake much activity so you conclude that you might as well not bother. In fact, motivation comes *after* action: once you force yourself into doing something then the motivation comes to sustain the action. Regular activity will help to improve your energy and mood levels. Therefore, don't make decisions on how you feel right now (for example, 'Lousy, and I want to go to bed') as you're likely to undermine your efforts to get better, but make them on how you want to feel ('More hopeful about things, so I'll push myself to go out for walk as I usually feel a bit better after that'). Thinking and acting against your depressive thoughts and beliefs helps you to overcome your feelings of helplessness ('There's nothing I can do') and hopelessness ('What's the point?') in order to begin to enjoy life again.

Anger

The central theme in anger is some form of perceived transgression against yourself either by others or when you do it to yourself (for example, 'Why the hell can't I keep my word when I give it?'). This transgression can occur in three main areas. First, when you're blocked or thwarted in some way from achieving an important goal (for example, 'Why the hell didn't those bastards give me the promotion. They know how hard I've worked for it'). Second, that important personal rules have been violated by others (for example, 'When I say "Good morning" to you, I expect the same courtesy from you – you ignorant git!') or yourself (for example, 'I can't control my weight. What's wrong with me?'). Third, when your self-esteem seems threatened in some way such as when you verbally insult your friend by calling him a 'scrooge' when he asks you for the return of his loan; in so doing, he has reminded you, intentionally or not, that you failed to have the money ready on the day you said you would and therefore your word can't be trusted.

When you're feeling angry you may verbally or physically lash out (retaliate) or, if deemed not to be an appropriate response in certain circumstances (for example, to your boss), displace your aggression on to someone or something else (such as by shouting at your partner or smashing crockery). Instead of attacking, you may withdraw from a situation as when you storm out of a meeting or relationship. You may be reluctant to get even with someone directly (for example, deriding your ex-partner's sexual inadequacy in front of his new girlfriend) but, instead, do it indirectly (by, for example, spreading rumours that he is gay). When this retaliation is expressed indirectly, it is known as passive-aggressiveness. Studies have demonstrated that prolonged anger and hostility increases the risk of coronary heart disease and other physical disorders (Chesney and Rosenman, 1985).

You may believe that letting your anger out is the best way to deal with it and you feel much better after this cathartic release (keeping it in will wreak internal havoc). In our experience, these cathartic expressions of anger only reinforce your anger because the beliefs underpinning it are strengthened rather than weakened, for example, you rant and rave about your partner leaving you but his 'treachery' lives on corrosively in your mind; you give a colleague a 'piece of my mind' and he replies in kind, exacerbating an already tense situation. As Leahy observes: 'Few people become less angry by becoming more angry' (1996: 44). You may believe that other people should change instead of yourself because they're the cause of your anger. However, you will remain stuck with your anger as it's highly unlikely that others will follow your dictates.

The most effective way for dealing with your anger is stated by Hauck: 'To get over being angry you must first get over the idea you have been taught all your life, namely, that *other people make you angry*' (1980: 37; emphasis in original). When you're faced with frustrating circumstances or people behaving badly, you have choices about how you wish to respond; if you blow your top rather than feel annoyed or irritated, it's because you have pressed your anger button ('I shouldn't be stuck in a bloody traffic jam when I've got to get to an important meeting!'). You may regret your behaviour later which shows that other options were available to you in that situation.

To reinforce our point, imagine waiting in a hospital outpatients' clinic for your appointment which is at 2 p.m. but it's now 3.30 p.m. What would you say to yourself to feel: (a) irritated (for example, 'It's a pain in the neck having to wait this long but I realise they have a lot of patients to see') and (b) very angry (for example, 'What the fucking hell are they doing keeping me hanging around like this? I haven't got all bloody day. Inefficient, useless bastards!'). This exercise can help you to establish the cause-and-effect relationship between your thoughts and feelings. Your self-talk determines the way you respond to a situation; therefore, any angry outburst is the result of your thinking about the situation, not the situation itself.

We're certainly not arguing that all anger is wrong or harmful. Instead, we encourage you to identify those situations where it could be or is having unwelcome consequences – such as in loving relationships, work performance or social life; and consider what alternative reactions you would like to adopt. These reactions could include: being more assertive, that is, standing up for yourself without being angry (see Chapter 7); developing an early warning system by recognizing the signs of incipient anger (for example, muscle tension, clenched fists, becoming impatient); and learning how to defuse it before it 'explodes' by talking yourself down or leaving the situation until you feel calmer. And fundamentally, pinpointing and changing the beliefs that drive your anger such as your demand that the world should run to your timetable and therefore you should not have to experience any inconvenience. Once you have calmed down, then you can decide how to deal with life's inevitable frustrations in a more constructive way.

Shame

Shame stems from your assumption that you have revealed publicly a defect, weakness, or inadequacy and that others will agree with your negative self-evaluation. For example, a person who prides himself on his emotional control flies into a rage when stuck in a long supermarket queue; other shoppers turn, stare at him and mutter among themselves. He imagines they think he is bad-tempered and out of control and therefore disapprove of him. As Lazarus points out: 'Shame is a discrepancy between what the person wants to be and the way that person is identified socially' (1999: 239).

When you feel ashamed, you want to remove yourself from the gaze of others or wish the 'ground to open up and swallow me'. If you can't withdraw from the situation, you may avoid eye contact or keep your head bowed to avoid what you think will be the harsh scrutiny of others. However, feeling trapped in the situation may increase your level of agitation and draw further attention to yourself. Once free of the situation, you may try to avoid going there again as you assume people will never forget your behaviour and point and stare at you when you return, for example, going back to the supermarket.

Sometimes you may feel embarrassed rather than ashamed. Embarrassment can be viewed as a much milder form of shame where weaknesses or flaws you reveal to others are not central to your social identity, for example, calling someone by the wrong name even though you have met him several times; in my (MN) case, giving a lecture to students who listened politely and then informed me ten minutes into the talk that I was in the wrong classroom. When embarrassed, you're able to poke fun at yourself (for example, 'I've got a head like a sieve. I'd forget my own name if it wasn't for my wife reminding me of it'), whereas in shame the character failure is usually too painful for any humour to be used.

So far we've focused on external shame (that is, revealing your imperfections to others and being judged negatively for them); you can also experience internal shame whereby you denigrate yourself for falling below 'some internalised ideal or standard' (Gilbert, 1998: 242). For example, when alone you drink heavily to cope with work-related stress and condemn yourself as weak for not being able to take 'stress in my stride like my colleagues'. Even alone, others are still psychologically present as you worry about them finding out about your shameful secret.

To start tackling shame, learn to separate your behaviour from yourself, for example, 'I may have acted foolishly but that does not make me a fool'; 'I'm drinking to cope with my stress which is not really helping me but that does not make me a weak person' (see above section on labelling). If these actions don't make you a fool or weak, what do they make you? We would argue that these actions are part of your fallibility and complexity as a human being and therefore it's futile to attach a label to yourself as this can never capture your totality as a human being (for example, if you're weak, then the only actions you can ever perform are weak ones; does that reflect the reality of your life?). If you stop putting yourself down on the basis of your actions, then you can also stop agreeing with others' actual or imagined negative evaluations of you (for example, 'You might see me as incompetent but I see myself as acting incompetently in certain situations which I'm trying to put right. I don't see myself as an incompetent person, so I'm not going to run away and hide because you see me that way'); in addition, you might try to determine whether people do view you negatively instead of naturally assuming that they do. Through these methods you can learn to feel disappointed about but not ashamed of your behaviour as you're now viewing events through the lens of compassionate self-acceptance – how you want to live in your own mind is now more important to you than how you want your public self to live in the minds of others (for example, always appearing strong).

An excellent way to change your shame-producing ideas is through shame-attacking exercises. These exposure exercises involve engaging in activities that will invite public ridicule or criticism (for example, asking directions to the local railway station while standing outside of it) while at the same time accepting yourself for your behaviour (for example, 'I may act stupidly and people laugh at me because of it, but that doesn't make me a stupid person'). Ensure that your chosen exercises don't involve breaking the law, violating your ethical standards, putting yourself or others in danger or bringing about self-defeating consequences such as losing your job or jeopardising your promotion chances. You will need to tolerate the intense anxiety you will probably feel in carrying out these exercises as well as providing yourself with some forceful coping statements to remain in the situation (for example, 'Put the shame to flight, not myself'). Also, you can learn that nothing terrible will happen to you if people laugh at or disapprove of you: it's the meaning you attach to the laughter or disapproval (for example, 'I've shown myself to be a complete idiot') rather than the laughter or disapproval itself which leads to your shameful feelings.

These exercises can act as a rehearsal before you carry them out in areas of your life where you wish to make changes (for example, speaking up in meetings or groups where previously you would have kept quiet for fear of saying something stupid; revealing things about yourself to friends or colleagues such as 'I used to be an alcoholic' because you're no longer afraid of rejection or hostile opinion). These exercises and the philosophy underpinning them can help to free you from the inhibitions of shame and the restrictions they place on your life.

Guilt

The theme in guilt is of a moral violation or lapse. You can feel guilty about actions that primarily affect yourself (for example, not keeping to your diet, having 'dirty' thoughts) or about the consequences of your actions which hurt or harm others. Your actions that affect others are usually divided into acts of commission (that is, what you have done), for example, 'My wife was devastated when she found out about my affair with her sister' and acts of omission (that is, what you have failed to do), for example, 'My mate was desperate to talk to someone about his worries but I couldn't be bothered to listen. Now he's in hospital after taking an overdose.' This division is also true for your actions not relevant to others, for example, 'I ate pork' (act of commission by an orthodox Jew) and 'I didn't pray today' (act of omission by a Muslim). Guilt and shame are often seen as interchangeable but they have similarities as well as differences. As Wessler and Wessler explain:

> [Guilt and shame] result from the same type of ideation and, as far as we can tell, produce the same type of arousal. Both involve doing something considered bad, stupid, or wrong. The difference is the locus of evaluation – external for shame, internal for guilt. Shame comes from receiving the disapproval of others; guilt, from receiving one's own disapproval. In both cases, the conclusion is 'I'm no good'.
>
> (1980: 96)

When feeling guilty you may try to right the wrong by, for example, begging forgiveness from the person you believe you have wronged or showering them with presents or affection or acting in an obedient manner (for example, 'I can't refuse her anything after the way I've behaved'); you may believe you deserve some form of punishment and administer it yourself (for example, overdose) or leave it to others (for example, being beaten up); you may attempt to anaesthetise yourself to the pain of guilt (for example, drink, drugs or overwork); you may forbid yourself any pleasure until you have expiated your sins. It's the 'over the top' nature of the behaviour that's the problem here.

Damning yourself as 'bad' or 'wicked' for violating your moral code may actually encourage you to continue to act in such ways as you neglect to try and understand why you behaved in that way in the first place; in other words, you act in accordance with your self-definition. A more constructive solution is to label your behaviour as 'wrong' or 'bad' (and explore the reasons for it and learn from your errors) but refrain from self-condemnation through self-forgiveness, for example, 'I know I behaved very badly at the time and I unreservedly apologise for it.' This is more likely to lead to a feeling of remorse for your actions but without guilt because you have avoided self-labelling. If other people are involved, you can explain to them 'why I did what I did', ask for forgiveness but not beg for it, engage in acts of reparation if appropriate (for example, a financial settlement). In these ways, a moral lapse becomes an episode in the story of your life, never the whole story.

You can also examine the 'should' statements in your moral standards: are they tyrannical, for example, 'I (absolutely) should never have a moral lapse but if I do this means I'm a bad person' or tolerant, for example, 'I (preferably) should never have a moral lapse but if I do, this means I'm a fallible human being who regrets his behaviour, not a damnable one based upon this moral lapse'. Tyrannical 'shoulds' are guilt-creating while tolerant 'shoulds' are more likely to generate remorse, that is, your conscience still pricks you, but not so painfully.

A key technique for tackling guilt is to assess your degree of responsibility for an adverse outcome instead of assuming it was *all* your fault. List all the people and factors relevant to the event and give each one a percentage rating (the total must not go above 100 per cent and put yourself last on the list). In the following example, Joan believed she was completely responsible for upsetting her husband when she forgot to buy him a birthday present. This was Joan's redistribution of responsibility:

1. 'My husband believes that as I forgot his birthday I don't love him anymore. This is totally untrue. Those are his ideas, not mine, so that explains why he reacted that way.' 60 per cent.
2. 'It was an extremely busy time at work and, unfortunately, his birthday slipped my mind.' 20 per cent.
3. 'I could have made a note in my diary to get a birthday present.' 20 per cent.

Redistributing responsibility (also known as reattribution) for events is not meant to get you 'off the hook' if you are primarily or totally responsible for an event (for example, knocking down a pedestrian through drunk driving) but to help you stand back from the event and apportion commensurate responsibility (with Joan's example, she no longer felt guilty, but regretted her oversight in forgetting her husband's birthday and apologised to him for it which he accepted). This technique is best done after you have addressed your guilt-inducing self-judgements and your 'should' statements as discussed above.

Hurt

When you feel hurt you're reacting to a perceived injustice perpetrated against you (for example, 'It's not fair that you always put yourself first instead of thinking of my needs sometimes'). You may assume that you have been let down or betrayed by another and conclude that you're undeserving of such treatment. Hurt can be blended with other emotions: self-pitying hurt – 'I only ever wanted you to love me. I didn't do anything wrong. Why are you treating me like this?', for example; depressed hurt – 'I must be worthless because of the way you're treating me'; angry hurt – 'You're a bastard for ignoring my feelings.'

When you're feeling hurt, you will often withdraw from the person who has hurt you and shut down verbal communication with him. This resentful silence or aloofness from others is often referred to as sulking. You can engage in silent sulking or angry sulking, for example, slamming doors around the house or you may snipe at your partner from time to time without revealing to him what you're hurt about (if he really loves you, then you assume he should know what he's done to upset you). With this behaviour, you hope to get even with or punish your partner in some way (for example, you attempt to induce guilt in him for his selfish behaviour and then he will ask you for your forgiveness) while avoiding a head-on confrontation. Lazarus suggests that sulking indicates a

> dependence on the other person's attentions and good will. The sulker does not dare make a strong attack lest the other person become totally alienated and the relationship endangered or lost. Sulking presents a picture of neediness, inadequacy, and even childishness.
>
> (1999: 227)

In order to overcome hurt, it's important to try and establish the facts of the situation. For example you might think, 'My wife has gone to bed early. I'll ask her if she's alright' rather than rely on your own interpretations of it ('She's gone to bed early because she's fed up with me. What did I do wrong?'). Even if you're being treated in an unfair or uncaring way there's no law of the universe or of parliament (except the law in your head) which states that you *must* not be treated in this manner or you *must* get what you believe you deserve (for example, to be appreciated at all times). Accepting this realistic attitude is more likely to lead to feeling disappointed in your partner's behaviour rather than hurt by it and, instead of sulking, assertively communicating to him what changes you would like to see in his behaviour, for example: 'I would greatly appreciate it if you would spend a few minutes talking to me when you come home from work instead of going directly to your post and newspapers first'. Time spent sulking could be more usefully employed in seeking improvements in your relationship. However, if you enjoy 'a bit of a sulk' make it time limited such as thirty minutes soaking in the bath and then engaging in an adult-to-adult conversation.

Jealousy

The theme in romantic jealousy is of an actual or imagined threat to your relationship posed by another (the rival). Morbid jealousy has been described 'as an excessive irrational preoccupation with the partner's fidelity for which there is no objective foundation' (Bishay *et al.*, 1996: 9). If you suffer from morbid jealousy, you may infer the following: that your partner's desertion is imminent; that threats exist to your relationship where none actually do; that conversations your partner is having with other men are evidence of her infidelity; that you no longer have the exclusive attention or love of your partner; and that your partner is acting in a way that violates your 'property' rights. Your jealousy is often combined with other emotions: for example, 'What if she leaves me? I can't survive without her' (anxiety); 'If she is attracted to someone else, then that proves I'm repulsive' (depression); 'I'll smash that bastard's head in for trying to take her away from me' (anger). Hauck (1982a) suggests that it's not the distrust of your partner that causes your jealousy but distrust of yourself: your perceived inability to cope with and see off actual or potential rivals because you're inferior to them (for example, not as attractive or inadequate in bed).

When you're morbidly jealous, you're likely to, inter alia, seek constant reassurance from your partner (for example, 'Do you really love me?'), monitor your partner's behaviour (for example, 'Did you say you went to the pub on Friday night, because my mate Joe said he never saw you there?'), check for signs of infidelity (for example, checking car seats for any tell-tale 'stains'), restrict your partner's movements (for example, 'I don't want you to go to that party on Saturday'), and continually accuse your partner of unfaithfulness (for example, 'Don't lie to me: I know you're seeing him'). The predictable result of such behaviour is to drive away the very person whom you profess to love so much – your partner!

In mild or moderate jealousy (or what Ellis, 1996, calls 'healthy amative heartburn'), you still infer that a threat exists to your relationship but use this threat as a stimulus to discover what may be going wrong in the relationship and seek to address it constructively (for example, your partner is fed up with your long working hours and lack of sex and you agree to spend more time with her both in and out of bed). You don't demand the exclusive attention of your partner because you realise that he can be attractive to other women (you may even feel proud that you're going out with someone who is so attractive to others) without ending up in bed with them.

If infidelity has occurred and you still want to save the relationship, then you can assertively state what new behaviours you expect from your partner and what the consequences will be if he backslides. If, in the final analysis, you're rejected by your partner, you don't have to reject yourself on the basis of his rejection, because your self-evaluation is in your hands, not his (for example, 'He may no longer fancy me but I can still pull if I choose to'). You choose to because relationships are enjoyable and not because your worth as a person depends on being loved. In this way, the ideas that stir morbid jealousy are not transferred to your next relationship.

Envy

When you're envious you desire (covet) the good fortune or advantages possessed by another. Lazarus (1999) suggests that envy can be distinguished from jealousy as the former involves two people (for example, 'Why does my brother get all the attractive women? I'm just as good looking as he is') whereas jealousy involves three people (for example, 'Why is that bloke chatting to my wife. Is he trying to seduce her or something?'). We distinguish between resentful and non-resentful envy.

In resentful envy (which may become malicious at times), you will often compare yourself unfavourably with the person who has what you want (for example, 'I try as hard as she does but she seems to have all the luck while I'm jinxed in some way'); you may denigrate in your mind the value of what you desire (for example, 'Admittedly, she's gorgeous but who wants to go out with an airhead? He can have her'); you may convince yourself that you're actually better off without the desired possession and even superior in some way (for example, 'Winning all that money is going to bring him nothing but grief. I don't envy him at all. In fact, I think you lead a more honest and balanced life without all that money being showered on you and inevitably corrupting you'); you may persuade yourself that what you have is just the same as or better than what the other person has (for example, 'Mine might be an older car but it will outlast that flashy pile of junk he's just bought'); you may tell yourself that you will get what the other person has whether or not you need it; and you may ponder on how to deprive the other person of the object of your desire (for example, 'That would wipe the smile off his face if I destroyed his lottery ticket so he couldn't collect his winnings'). Finally, you find enjoyment in the misfortunes of others particularly if they're rich, attractive, famous, talented or successful – 'How the mighty have fallen, and about time too!'

Your envious thoughts may lead you to act on them by telling the other person what you think of him or his possessions/advantages, by trying to take away the desired possession or by destroying or spoiling it in some way. Gilbert (1989) remarks that envy is rife in competitive cultures where individualism, material gain and success are emphasised. Admitting envy may lead you to feel ashamed because others may see you as mean-spirited or a loser; therefore, you will usually deny that you feel envious.

When you feel non-resentful envy, you will honestly and often openly express your desire for what the other person has but without denigrating her or the desired possession; you may ask her for advice on how to get for yourself what she has (for example, 'I've always admired your success with men. Any tips on how I can improve my success rate?'); you may genuinely express your support to her for obtaining what you wanted (for example, 'You got the promotion. Well done') or genuinely commiserate with her misfortunes instead of gloating over them (for example, 'I'm sorry your business failed. It takes a lot of guts to strike out on your own').

Try not to convince yourself that you're happy with what you have when, in fact, you want to emulate her success (for example, 'I would like to write a book too'), or not having what she has somehow makes you superior. If you want the desired possession, then ensure it's for your own pleasure and not to prove 'what you can get, so can I'. With this new outlook, you no longer want to deprive her, in thought or deed, of her possessions because you allow her in your mind to have them. You realise that depriving her of them only brings you short-term satisfaction when you see her suffer, but reminds you in the longer term of your own feelings of resentment and inferiority.

While another person may have some or many of the qualities, circumstances, or possessions that you desire, trying to improve your own position in life is more constructive than attempting to destroy or undermine someone else's.

Conclusion

When you encounter emotional difficulties, remember the dictum: you feel as you think. Tap into your internal self-talk and, as we have shown, identify, challenge and change those aspects of your thinking that perpetuate these difficulties (as the saying goes, the thinking you stick with is the thinking you're stuck with). Maintaining change means continually putting into practice your new ideas and behaviours and monitoring yourself for signs of slipping back (which usually means the resurfacing of old self- and goal-defeating ideas). In other words, you will need to become your own lifelong coach if you want to deal successfully with your troublesome emotions.

Chapter 2

Problem-creating versus problem-solving

Introduction

What is a problem? This can be defined as facing a particular difficulty without having found an effective solution. Problems can be of a practical nature (difficulties with fractious colleagues) or of an emotional nature (guilt about being off work with illness); these two elements, the practical and emotional, frequently overlap. For example, a person who is depressed (emotional problem) about losing his job (practical problem) sees himself as a failure; this self-image is reinforced by his reluctance to look for another job. He gradually withdraws from others and takes solace in heavy alcohol use. This example can be seen as one of problem-creation, that is, the person's initial difficulties are added to by the adoption of a counterproductive strategy (though the person's internal experience might suggest it's the right response to make in the circumstances).

In the stress management/problem-solving literature, two important forms of coping have been described: problem-focused coping and emotion-focused coping (see Lazarus and Folkman, 1984). Problem-focused coping tackles stressful situations in order to change or modify them while emotion-focused coping addresses the emotional upset associated with these situations. If a situation is viewed as unchangeable, then emotion-focused coping is the most realistic strategy to pursue. This is achieved by helping the individual to alter the meaning he attaches to a situation (in the above example, the person decides that losing his job is part of the short-term contract culture rather than as a result of personal deficiencies). When problem-creating is replaced by successful problem-solving this leads to fewer difficulties experienced both internally and externally.

Problem-solving approaches are usually two-pronged because as Walen *et al.* observe:

Dealing with the emotional problem is necessary, but *not necessarily sufficient:* resolving emotional problems gets rid of emotional disturbance; dealing with *practical* problems leads to self-actualisation and improvement in the person's quality of life. Both are important.

(1992: 52; italics in original)

While individuals may have combinations of emotional and practical problems, in the following coaching examples we have focused on emotional problem-solving with the first person and practical problem-solving with the second.

Problem-creating: Paul

Paul worked for a large insurance company. His problems started one Monday afternoon when his manager asked him to have a report on her desk by midday on Friday. He revealed his anger when she was out of ear- and eyeshot: 'As if I haven't got enough bloody work to do already!' He was consumed by his anger for the rest of the afternoon and, as a consequence, little of his existing workload was dealt with.

He took his anger home, provoked a row with his wife and was sharp with his children. He had little sleep that night as he was still angry with his boss and felt guilty and ashamed because of his behaviour towards his family. The next day at work he was very tired and still seething with resentment because of the extra work he had been given; also, he was still brooding on his 'despicable' behaviour from last night. He now had to grapple with catching up on yesterday's work and continued to feel anxious because he had not started on the report. Little productive work was accomplished that day; as he said, 'my mind and emotions were all over the place. Am I losing it or something?'

He vowed to make some preliminary notes about the content of the report after the evening meal but, because he was so tired, fell asleep in a chair while watching television. Despite sleeping all night, he said he didn't feel refreshed the next morning. He had a busy day ahead of him but was preoccupied with his inability to start the report he had to deliver in a little over twenty-four hours' time. That evening he decided to go for broke and worked through the night to produce the report and kept his family awake in the process. At the office the next day he described himself as the 'walking dead' but delivered his report on schedule, but that afternoon he had to chair an important interdepartmental meeting and kept stifling yawns as well as trying to stop his head nodding and eyes closing. Over the weekend, instead of winding down, Paul was on tenterhooks about the quality of his report ('I expect it's dreadful') and his chairmanship of the meeting ('They probably thought I was on drugs or something'). Relief set in on Monday when his manager said the report was satisfactory and the feedback from the meeting was generally positive apart from his obvious tiredness. Even though Paul was more relaxed and could now focus on his work, he was very troubled as to how he'd gone 'out of control' the previous week.

Problem analysis

In reviewing Paul's work record, he was prone to creating problems about problems (that is, generating additional problems for yourself [PAP] because you have not tackled the primary problem [PP] constructively) and the aforementioned example was just the most spectacular case to date. In trying to demonstrate vividly this process, I (MN) wrote on the whiteboard in my office:

Primary Problem (PP):	angry about having to write a report in addition to his normal heavy workload
Problems about Problems (PAP):	falling behind with his workload
	prolonged anger
	preoccupation with thoughts of losing control
	guilty and ashamed about his behaviour towards his family
	lack of sleep
	rising anxiety
	working through the night
	chairing meeting in a very tired state
	unable to wind down over the weekend

Very soon the whiteboard was covered with Paul's succession of problems. Paul's response was: 'I see so clearly now the train of events, but why didn't I just have a quick temper tantrum, then make a start on the report? I had no problems actually writing the report' (if Paul had difficulties with this or other tasks, then learning some practical problem-solving skills could have supplemented emotional problem solving). By using the ABC model of emotional upset, Paul was able to pinpoint the upset-producing thinking that unleashed his disastrous week. I wrote the model on the whiteboard using Paul's answers to my questions:

A – activating event: asked to write a report in addition to his current heavy workload.

B – upset-creating beliefs: 'She shouldn't be doing this to me when I've got enough work to do already! I'm not bloody well doing it! She shouldn't be snowing me under with all this crap – it's not fair!'

C – emotional and behavioural consequences: anger, increasing agitation and decreasing work productivity.

This simple but insightful model states that it is our self- and task-defeating beliefs at B, not unpleasant or stressful events at A, that largely determine our upsetting emotional and behavioural reactions at C; in other words, A contributes to C but does not cause it.

So why did Paul get into such an emotional tangle? By not dealing with the primary problem (some might prefer the term challenge) when presented with it; namely, making a start on the report. Once he decided to avoid it or defiantly not do it, the problems about problems process started:

PAUL: When you put it up there on the board, it seems so clear now. Writing reports is part of my job – my boss didn't really ask me to do anything out of the ordinary. I suppose she just asked me at the wrong moment and everything spiralled out of control.

MICHAEL: Well, you let it spiral out of control because of that statement (pointing at the board) 'She shouldn't be doing this to me . . .' and what was it she was actually doing to you at that precise moment?

PAUL: She was asking me to do the report but, like a dog with a bone, I wouldn't let go of the idea that she shouldn't be doing what she was doing.

MICHAEL: And as soon as any individual starts to deny the reality of their situation, problems can start and then quickly escalate.

PAUL: That's exactly what happened to me. I just wouldn't let go of my anger – how dare she give me more work! The thing is though, I want to perform well under pressure because I'm looking for promotion. In fact, it's a funny thing: actually doing the report in the end caused me much less hassle than avoiding it.

MICHAEL: Good point. This is frequently the case: a difficult, boring or unpleasant task may take just an hour or two to complete but often individuals will spend hours, days, weeks or even longer avoiding it.

PAUL: It's crazy when I think about it. I thought my boss was doing my head in with the report when all the time it was me.

MICHAEL: Obviously if you thought you had legitimate grievances about the workload then it would be important to talk to your boss about this issue.

PAUL: Absolutely, but without the anger. Otherwise the problems about problems stuff will start again.

Problem-solving

Michael Bernard states that 'in order for you to think clearly and thus effectively handle stressful situations and solve practical problems, you first have to develop emotional control. *Emotional self-management is a vital key to stress management*' (1993, section III: 1; emphasis in original). This is achieved by modifying or changing the ideas and beliefs that largely create your emotional and behavioural reactions to events. Thus Paul was taught the additional elements of the ABC model: namely, disputing (D) his upset-creating beliefs with the use of reality-testing (that is, are your beliefs consistent with empirical reality or reality as it actually is at any given moment?) and pragmatism (that is, do your beliefs and behaviours help or hinder you in achieving your goals?). Through successful disputing of these beliefs, you develop a more rational or personally effective (E) philosophy of living accompanied by a level of emotional arousal (that is, non-upsetting) which is compatible with effective problem-solving. Paul had clung to reality-denying and upset-creating 'shoulds' for several days (and in previous work-related cases) which became the target for further exploration.

Horney (1950) spoke of the 'tyranny of the shoulds' (internal pressurisers) which dictate how self, others or the world should be (for example, 'I should be rewarded and respected for my hard work'). Of course, the word *should* is not itself either problem-creating or problem-solving; this is determined by the meaning embedded within the word: in Paul's case, shoulds that deny reality ('She shouldn't be doing this to me . . .'). As Paul wanted to manage the pressures of the workplace more effectively, he learnt to accept empirical reality at any given moment ('It should be happening to me because it is!') without necessarily having to like or approve of what he'd accepted. This is a good example of 'shoulds' that acknowledge empirical reality. What aided the development of Paul's new outlook was my (MN) use of DiGiuseppe's motivational syllogism (a syllogism is an argument in which a conclusion is deduced from several premises). The first premise is:

My present anger is dysfunctional (or counterproductive). The second premise is: There is an alternative script (new ways of thinking, feeling and behaving) that is more functional. The third premise is: I can control which reaction I have to the activating event. The conclusion is: I need to examine ways in which I can change my emotional reaction. (1995: 148)

Also, it's very important to understand that acceptance of reality does not mean being passive, resigned or indifferent to events but is the starting point to examine ways of changing or modifying these events. Therefore, when I focused on Paul's anger, I asked not whether it was justified in the circumstances but what were the consequences for him in holding on to his anger (for example, tasks took longer to complete). This approach usually yields a more productive outcome than challenging the basis of a person's anger as the latter strategy can reinforce the 'rightness' of their anger by the person's insistent defence of it. By examining the self-defeating, family-disrupting and task-blocking consequences of his anger, Paul was more likely to initiate self-change. If he was to give up his anger though, what feeling was going to take its place?

Paul's plan of action

As Paul wanted to avoid the disastrous chain of events that unfolded when he got angry about having to write the report, he left a message on his desk, prominently displayed, which read: 'When it happens, deal with it.' The 'it' could refer to any task, crisis, or setback. By gradually internalising this new attitude, he realised he could control his emotional reactions to workplace events; instead of anger he now experienced what he called a 'get on with it irritability'. He cited an example of being an eleventh-hour replacement to chair a meeting:

PAUL: Six months earlier if I'd been asked I would have got myself into a right old angry state, you know saying things like 'I shouldn't be put in this position' and 'They should have given me adequate warning' and so on.

MICHAEL: And now . . .?

PAUL: Well, I wasn't exactly overjoyed at the prospect but I immediately swung into action by quickly reviewing the background information to the key agenda items. This info came off the fax and I was reading it on the way to the meeting. Things went pretty smoothly. My manager thanked me for doing a good job. The secret I've discovered is to get hold of the problem straightaway and do something about it.

MICHAEL: And what if you can't do something about it straightaway . . .?

PAUL: Well, I'll just put it on hold until I can do something about it or accept the situation if I can't do anything about it at all. Whichever way it goes, I no longer get stressed out about it . . . most of the time. Rome wasn't built in a day, you know.

MICHAEL: And if you did get really stressed out, would you say at that point something like 'I shouldn't get stressed out now as I've learnt to handle things differently'?

PAUL: *(laughs)* No, I would say 'I am stressed out' which would acknowledge the reality of how I feel and then that would act as a self-administered kick up the backside to get myself back under control. It would be nice not to get stressed out or angry in the first place.

MICHAEL: Unlikely though. Remember, emotional self-management doesn't mean you will never get upset again but that you can greatly reduce its frequency, intensity and duration.

PAUL: I'll settle for that.

Problem-creating: Diana

Diana had changed careers in order to train as a stress-management counsellor. Since her training ended, she had not applied to any local companies for work. She wanted to feel 'really confident' before undertaking any stress management work and 'ensure that I made the right career change by not failing'. She knew that gaining confidence and becoming successful were more likely to occur *after* a period of sustained effort, not before it; however, as these outcomes could not be guaranteed, she felt stymied by her need for certainty. She decided that some further training 'might do the trick' but the hoped for confidence did not materialise. She couldn't afford these courses as the 'money was going out but nothing coming in'.

Diana saw her new career slipping away before it even got started: she was becoming paralysed by inaction. She even thought of returning to her old job: 'I suppose I could slink back as a failure.' What compounded her disappointment in herself was seeing some of her colleagues on the original course now getting some industrial work: 'Why them and not me?' She considered herself a poor role model as a stress-management counsellor because she wasn't handling her present problems in a constructive and realistic way: 'How can I teach stress management to others when I can't seem to solve my own problems.' She knew that 'make or break' time was not far away as financial pressures were mounting.

Problem analysis

Diana's difficulties were viewed within the framework of the ADAPT problem-solving model (Nezu *et al.*, 2007):

A – attitude

After much head-scratching in search of an optimistic attitude, Diana said she was 'prepared to give it all she's got'.

D – defining the problem and setting realistic goals

Diana described her problem as having 'no confidence in myself as a stress-management counsellor'. Butler and Hope (2007) suggest reformulating problems in terms that suggest they can be solved rather than remain unsolvable.

MICHAEL: Have you had confidence in yourself before?

DIANA: Of course, and I can give you plenty of examples, but it seems to have deserted me in this instance. I really want to succeed so much because I've burnt my bridges in changing careers.

MICHAEL: Is it success you're worried about, though?

DIANA: No, it's failing. That's what's holding me back.

MICHAEL: Can you state your problem in terms which indicate that progress can be made?

DIANA: Well, something like how to develop confidence in myself as a stress management counsellor.

MICHAEL: What about the failure part?

DIANA: I suppose see setbacks and failures as part of the learning experience.

MICHAEL: And what has your learning experience taught you so far?

DIANA: If I don't make a start soon, I will definitely fail in my new career.

During the problem-defining stage, your strengths, abilities and problem-solving skills can be noted down in order to determine whether you will be able to use the problem-solving model at the present time (if you're too emotionally upset you can use the ABCDE model to combat and change your upset-producing thinking before you refocus on the ADAPT model). If you have trouble defining your problem, it may be useful to state your goals and then work backwards to pinpoint what is stopping you from achieving them.

Goals need to be stated in specific and behavioural terms that allow for measurement of your progress, so, in Diana's case, 'I want to make three job applications per week over the next month.' Vague or unrealistic goals should be avoided, for example, 'I want things to be better' and 'I don't want to feel any anxiety'. Goals should also be within your area of control rather than outside of it, for example, 'I want my colleague to take on more of the work rather than dump it on me all the time' means that the responsibility for achieving the goal rests with the 'work avoidance' colleague who is hardly likely to comply! That person's goal, within her control, might be: 'I want to learn to be assertive so I can challenge my colleague about this issue and hopefully bring about some changes in the distribution of workloads.' Diana defined her goal as 'getting some paid work as a stress management counsellor within the next three months' which she saw as realistic:

MICHAEL: Who actually gives you the work?

DIANA: The employer, the company.

MICHAEL: So is that within your control?

DIANA: No.

MICHAEL: What is within your control?

DIANA: Letting people, companies know that I exist. Pushing myself forward, marketing myself. That can be the start of gaining confidence. Doing rather than stewing.

MICHAEL: So how many contacts do you hope to make per week, per month?

DIANA: I want to aim for six contacts per week over the first month.

A – generating alternative solutions

This step involves you generating as many solutions as possible to reach your goals no matter how ludicrous some of them initially appear; in other words, to brainstorm or let your imagination rip (evaluation of their potential usefulness comes later). If you find it difficult to get started on this process, ask a friend to suggest some possible solutions to you. If this block occurs in our coaching sessions, we may suggest to our clients some wild or extreme ideas to nudge their thinking along, for example, 'Ask a hundred women out in the next week.' Clients' usual responses to such ideas are to suggest more moderate ones (for example, 'Maybe one or two rather than a hundred'). Diana's solutions were:

(a) 'Blitz every company in the country with my CV and brochure.'
(b) 'Only concentrate on local companies and follow up my stuff with a phone call to introduce myself.'
(c) 'Talk to my colleagues and find out how they got their foot in the door.'
(d) 'Offer my services to local voluntary groups and organisations like the Women's Institute and the Rotary Club.'
(e) 'Send my stuff to local health authorities, education and social services departments, GP surgeries, gyms.'
(f) 'Put a leaflet through everybody's door in my neighbourhood.'

P – predicting the consequences and developing a solution plan

This involves you considering the advantages and disadvantages of each solution produced from the brainstorming session and the likely consequences of implementing each solution. You may wish to rate the usefulness of each possible solution on a scale from zero to ten (zero being the least useful to ten being most useful). Diana considered her solutions thus:

(a) 'I'm not ready for this and the costs would be prohibitive. Ruled out.' 0
(b) 'This seems more realistic but I would be worried about my lack of experience and therefore I don't think I would be value for money at this stage.' 4
(c) 'Good idea. I'm bound to get some sound advice.' 6
(d) 'This strikes me as the best way forward at the present time: I'd be getting much-needed practice and feedback, though no money yet, and maybe they won't be as tough an audience as I imagine they might be in business and industry. I'm sure this is the way to break through my lack of confidence barrier.' 8
(e) The same reservations as at solution two.' 4
(f) 'Only if I get really desperate.' 1

You now choose the most feasible or promising solution(s) which appear to have the fewest disadvantages and seem most likely to help you achieve your stated goals. Diana chose solutions (c) and (d). This step also involves means–ends thinking, that is, planning a series of steps in order to execute the chosen solution to achieve your goals. For example, if a person's goal is to stand up for himself in difficult social situations then he might need to learn assertion skills, rehearse these skills before carrying them out in the target situation, anticipate obstacles and plan how to overcome them (if he gets a hostile reception, does he want to revert to his previously passive state in these situations?).

T – trying out the solution to see if it works

Diana went to the library and looked on the Internet for lists of local voluntary organisations and started contacting them with offers of a stress management presentation; in some cases, she followed this up with a visit. Three groups accepted her offer, but she was still worried about her 'lack of practice' and suggested a solution to this that had not occurred to her at the generating alternative solutions stage: could she give a presentation to me (MN) as part of her coaching sessions? I agreed and brought in some of my colleagues to give her a bigger audience. We gave her a balanced and honest appraisal of her presentation; she was both grateful for the evaluation and relieved that 'I've now got one under my belt'. As Hauck emphasises, this is how self-confidence develops:

> You never fail as long as you are trying. Each trial teaches you something *if* you study your behaviour. You're getting valuable feedback from each effort, and this information is a small segment of success. Don't knock it. If you repeat the trials often enough, you add up little successes until they become noticeable. The upshot is that you are failing *only* when you are not trying, never otherwise.
>
> (1982b: 60; italics in original)

Diana was taught coping imagery whereby she imagined getting mostly negative feedback for a presentation and seeing this as an opportunity for learning and improvement instead of condemning herself and giving up. She agreed to carry out this imagery exercise on a daily basis in the run-up to her presentations as part of 'Diana's Development Programme'.

Review of progress

So, has progress been made and your goal been achieved? If not, what obstacles did you find difficult to overcome? Was it the right solution? Did you persist enough or did you give up too quickly? Are there further skills you need to acquire to make goal-attainment more likely? Finding a satisfactory solution to your problems is usually a combination of trial and error and persistence (see Chapter 5 for a discussion of persistence).

Diana said that her three presentations to local voluntary agencies went 'reasonably well' and she felt more confident. She said that the next stage was 'to get my foot in the door of local companies and start making some money'. To that end, she chose solution (b) generated earlier. 'Picking the brains' of her colleagues had yielded some good ideas that she would use in her own 'getting through the door' efforts. Diana concluded that 'confidence comes in small steps through struggle, not in a cocoon of comfort and the great near-effortless leaps that I wanted'. Diana was learning to become her own problem-solver. A follow-up coaching session with Diana established that she'd secured one paying client within the three month period she'd set herself.

If your solution has, for whatever reason, proved ineffective you can pick another one from the list in the generating solutions stage or brainstorm new ones based on what you've learnt from your experiences or ask friends and colleagues for ideas. Once you gain proficiency at using the ADAPT model, you may want a shorter model for rapid processing of a problem in order to deal with a crisis or make a quick decision; if so, try PIE (with this model, you may experience a less satisfactory outcome than with ADAPT because deliberation is exchanged for speed):

P – Problem definition
I – ideas for problem-solving and implementing chosen ones
E – evaluation of outcome

Conclusion

Problem-creating is easily done. One form discussed in this chapter is reality-denying 'should' statements which frequently lead to emotional upsets and the generation of additional problems. The antidote to this kind of thinking is suggested by Walen *et al.*:

> Accepting an unfortunate reality and not getting overly upset about it acknowledges that the reality exists, that it is unpleasant, that it would be irrational to demand or insist that it should not have happened, and that we will attempt to change it, if we can.
>
> (1992: 22)

Our second example of problem-creating focused on a person's lack of confidence about achieving success in her new career; she wanted to feel confident before seeking work yet knew that confidence comes from performance, not in the absence of it. By following a practical problem-solving model, she was encouraged to systematically think her way through to identifying, implementing and evaluating some confidence-building activities.

Whether your problems are emotional or practical, or a combination of the two, we hope that these two models of problem-solving will help you in their resolution.

Chapter 3

Overcoming procrastination

Introduction

A common dictionary definition of procrastination is 'to defer action', that is, to decide deliberately to do something later on (for example, 'I have deferred my decision until next Wednesday'). This is an example of planned delay in order to consider all the available evidence before making the decision. When individuals have problems with procrastination, however, it usually refers to them acting in a dilatory manner and thus laying something aside until a future unspecified time (for example, 'I will do it eventually'); or, if a future time has been specified, no action occurs when the time arrives (for example, 'I was going to start the essay today but a friend popped round and one thing led to another'). To put the problem of procrastination simply: you keep putting off doing what your better judgement tells you ought to be done now (incidentally, procrastinate is often confused with prevaricate which means 'to act or speak evasively or misleadingly'). Sometimes procrastination is accompanied by self-condemnation (for example, 'I want to knuckle down but I'm useless at doing it').

What holds you back?

What blocks you from engaging in productive action? Hauck suggests that poor self-discipline is an unsurprising human trait as 'avoiding a difficult situation seems like the most natural course to take because we are so easily seduced by immediate satisfactions' (1982b:18). Procrastination is often a behavioural way of protecting yourself from experiencing an unpleasant emotional state (for example, you prefer to watch television instead of starting on your pile of paperwork; if you do start you will experience intense irritation and boredom). A form of procrastination which might be difficult to detect is the 'comfort of discomfort' paradox:

your current lethargic or non-productive state is familiar and safe compared with the feared consequences of change and subsequent failure. Therefore, your claim that 'I'm happy the way that I am' is not so much a statement of genuine contentment but a fear of being even worse off if the change process fails. Hence you decide to stay in your rut rather than attempt to leave it.

Causes of procrastination

Dryden and Gordon (1993) identify three main causes of procrastination:

1. Anxiety

This is based on perceived threats to your self-esteem if you engage in the avoided task. Some examples: imagine asking someone out for a date instead of avoiding it. The prospect of doing so creates anxiety as you believe she will say no and thus confirm your unattractiveness. You continually put off writing an article because you fear it will be rejected for publication thereby proving 'I have no talent'. You loaf around the house instead of working on your college essay; you fear you won't get a top grade and will be exposed as average instead of exceptional. Avoiding these activities helps to keep your anxiety and the associated feared consequences 'out of sight' in the short term but perpetuates your problems in the longer term, for example, no romantic activity.

2. Low frustration tolerance (LFT)

This refers to your perceived inability to endure frustration, boredom, hard work, uncomfortable feelings, setbacks, so unpleasant tasks are avoided or quickly given up when started. The philosophical core of LFT is: 'I can't stand present pain for future gain.' For example, you want to become fit but the effort involved is 'too much' you declare and thereby resign yourself to staying unfit. A friend of mine (MN) a number of years ago won a holiday for two in Barbados but he was required by the travel company to go London to fill in some forms. He told me he could not be bothered with 'all the hassle' and consequently he lost the holiday. His partner hit the roof, told him it was typical of his general attitude and then walked out on him. LFT is a deceptive philosophy because it encourages you to think you're winning by avoiding unpleasant tasks or situations whereas your life actually becomes much harder in the long run as your unresolved problems mount up.

3. Rebellion

This is used as a way of expressing your anger towards others by delaying important tasks – you want to get back at someone for being told what to do or how to behave. Let's look at some examples. Your partner keeps on at you to make sure that your tax returns are sent in before the deadline. However, you resent being spoken to 'as if I'm a child' and deliberately miss the deadline 'to show her', but you incur a financial penalty which you dislike having to pay. Your boss tells you to carry out some additional work for him; you bristle with indignation at being treated like 'his bloody slave' and your 'I'll show him' attitude results in poor-quality work and missed deadlines. Your 'bolshie' attitude is noted and leads to you not being considered for promotion. Your desire to get back at others often rebounds on you.

Anxiety, LFT and rebellion may all be found in a single instance of procrastination. For example, your boss tells you to get back to her with a date for a workshop she wants you to run on improving workplace performance. You procrastinate over nominating a date because you're angry with her for 'dumping this job on me instead of buying in professionals to do it'. Your procrastination also involves a great distaste for all the preparatory work you will have to do for the workshop as well as your fear that it will be a flop and you will be exposed as incompetent.

People who regularly procrastinate often delay in three major areas: self-development, personal maintenance and honouring commitments to others (Dryden, 2000). Self-development refers to attempts to realise desired goals, for example, changing one's job or career, seeking new partners, developing an exciting social life. Personal maintenance involves undertaking tasks which make life easier, for example, doing housework, paying bills on time, answering correspondence, repairing the car. Honouring commitments to others are promises made earlier, sometimes in good faith or because you have trouble saying no, but which you now regret making and see as burdens (for example, 'Blast it! Why didn't I keep my mouth shut about helping him to move'). Instead of honouring your commitment, you hope he will have forgotten about it, offer lame excuses why you can't help him or you act forgetful if he brings it up.

Some surveys suggest that up to 20 per cent of the adult population are chronic procrastinators and suffer the usually high costs for such behaviour:

It [procrastination] has been associated with depression, guilt, low exam grades, anxiety, neuroticism, irrational thinking, cheating and low self-esteem. As a result, procrastination probably accounts for much of why many never realize their full potential and so it can be an extremely disabling psychological condition.

(Persaud, 2005: 237)

Putting things off

Avoidance behaviours and the rationalisations (also known as excuses) that accompany them can include the following:

- Contemplating the task at hand without actually engaging in it, for example, sitting in an armchair for long periods thinking about putting up shelves, 'I need to get the feel of a job before I actually start it.' Armchair contemplation will not help you get the 'feel' of a task, but doing it will.
- Leaving tasks until the last minute because 'I do my best work under pressure'. To verify this claim, you would need to compare the quality of your 'last minute' work with your 'starting earlier' work. This might trigger the real problem such as the sheer, boring grind of working longer on the task. Working under pressure means you have 'to rush to complete it, cannot assemble all the relevant materials to help you do it well, have little time to look it over and review it, and often have to polish it off in a relatively unfinished, glossed-over manner' (Ellis and Knaus, 1977:137).
- Claiming 'I'll do it tomorrow' and then trying to convince yourself that you mean it or that 'the job is as good as done'. In reality, tomorrow is not the next day but a hazy point in time in the distant future. Like the pub sign which says 'Free beer tomorrow', the promise of action tomorrow is not fulfilled. Action today can mean less worry and more opportunities tomorrow. Next time you say 'I'll do it tomorrow' instead of confirming your assertion that the task can only be done at a later date, prove yourself wrong by starting the task now!
- Making future action contingent upon present problem-solving, for example, 'I'll start asking women out when I've lost a bit of weight and have had a few sessions at the gym so I can feel better about myself.' This is a variation on the 'I'll do it tomorrow' theme. Diverting yourself into these activities, weight loss and getting fitter, which may be undertaken half-heartedly or not at all, keeps you from facing your real problem – in this instance, fear of rejection followed by self-rejection ('Women don't fancy a slob like me').

- Finding that previously unimportant tasks suddenly become all-important thereby pushing the unpleasant task into the background, for example, 'The house needs a spring clean. I can't be expected to fill in all this paperwork sitting in a dirty house.' If the unpleasant task was to magically disappear, would the house still need an urgent spring clean?

- Undertaking pleasurable pursuits first as a way of encouraging you to face the difficult task eventually. The pleasures then linger thereby pushing the task back to another time: 'Why spoil a good thing? There's plenty of time to cut the grass on another day.' Of course, you can enjoy yourself and cut the grass on the same day.

- Being continually alert to any seemingly plausible reason to resist starting or desisting from the task, for example, 'The phone's ringing and it could be an important call. My husband could be in trouble.' Once the phone call is finished, you may look for other ways to distract yourself from the task (for example, having a cup of coffee, writing out a shopping list) or tell yourself that you've lost your momentum to continue with it. You could force yourself back into the task and surprise yourself at how quickly you can recover your momentum.

- Creating the illusion of tackling the task, that is, to all intents and purposes you're carrying out work that seems to be a precursor to the task itself, for example, tidying your desk and room before settling down to type your essay on the computer. However, once the preparatory work is done – 'A tidy room is a tidy mind' – you consider that you have done enough for the time being; actually typing the essay, or at least beginning it, is avoided but you convince yourself that you have 'made a start on it' and can now turn your mind to something more pleasurable. Illusions can be comforting but they don't complete essays for you. We call doing such tasks 'pseudo-work' as it is not really part of the job to be done but you persuade yourself that it is.

- Calling yourself 'lazy', 'a slow starter' or 'a hopeless case' allows you to justify your procrastination as well as deflect criticism from others who complain about your tardiness, for example, 'I can't help it if I'm a lazy git.' If you were to stop hiding behind your name-calling and got down to business, you might experience the real problem – not your laziness but, for example, the fear of failure fuelling your procrastination.

- Waiting to feel motivated before you start a task as you reason with yourself that you can hardly be expected to carry out a difficult task in an unmotivated state or if you're not in the right mood. As Burns points out: 'Motivation doesn't come first – productive action does. You have to prime the pump by getting started whether you feel like it or not. Once you begin to accomplish something, it will often spur you on to do even more.' (1989: 170)

- Telling yourself to 'let sleeping dogs lie' even though you feel aggrieved about your partner's selfish behaviour. To confront him about his behaviour might lead to feared consequences (for example, he leaves you). Therefore, you delay asserting yourself 'until the right moment arrives'. That moment is unlikely to arrive unless you 'wake the dogs up'.

People can also procrastinate over things that could benefit them rather than have negative consequences. When people say they're afraid of success this can mean initial success followed by subsequent failure: they cannot see success lasting; they will feel uncomfortable at the prospect of success because they believe they don't deserve it; or their idea of what success means does not sit well with their self-image or values, for example, 'I'm not the kind of person who wants to get on at the expense of others. Success is a zero-sum game.' Such individuals may fall well short of realising their full potential.

Typology of procrastinators

Sapadin and Maguire (1996: 10) state that 'essentially, procrastination is caused by an internal conflict' and have identified six fundamental procrastination styles:

The perfectionist

You're reluctant to start or finish tasks because you might not achieve your uncompromisingly high standards. Therefore, you may find excuses to explain your less-than -perfect performance in order to avoid self-condemnation, for example, 'I didn't get a grade A for the exam because I was partying too much. If I'd done some serious studying and got less than an A, then I really would be a failure.'

The dreamer

You have a tendency towards vagueness and lack of realism; grandiose ideas are not translated into achievable goals. You use fantasy as an escape from the dreariness or seemingly unchangeable pattern of your life.

The worrier

You fear things going wrong and being overwhelmed by events; there-fore, you avoid risk or change and have little confidence in your ability to make decisions or tolerate discomfort.

The crisis-maker

You like to display bravado in declaring you can't get motivated until the eleventh hour or this is when you do your best work. Living 'on the edge' gives you an adrenaline rush. You usually exhibit a very low threshold for boredom. Alternatively, in eleventh-hour procrastination, you hope the task will miraculously disappear or someone will appear to help you with it or do it for you.

The defier

Either you're aggressive and argumentative towards others' suggestions or instructions because this means you're being told what to do or that other people are trying to control you; or you're passive-aggressive in style and say yes when you mean no as a means of indirectly getting back at someone else because you're afraid or reluctant to voice your true feelings.

The over-doer

You're always working on something and often making extra work for yourself, yet you don't focus on the important issues that need to be tack-led (for example, deciding what your real goals and values are in life). You have difficulty saying no and delegating work.

The common denominator of procrastination

According to Dryden and Gordon, the 'one thing all people who pro-crastinate have in common . . . is a clear-cut emotional problem' (1993: 59). You may not be aware of your own emotional problem because your avoidance behaviour (also known as safety behaviour) protects you from experiencing it. The way to 'release' this emotion is to face the avoided situation, in imagination or reality, and identify the beliefs and thoughts maintaining the procrastination. The ABC model of emotional problems helps you to understand this process:

A – activating event: you imagine asking questions and making comments at a meeting (instead of keeping silent or saying very little which is your usual pattern of behaviour)

B – beliefs and thoughts: 'I'll say the wrong thing or get my facts confused and look an idiot in the eyes of others'

C – emotional consequences: intense anxiety

Exposing yourself in imagination to what you normally avoid (A) triggers but does not cause your intense anxiety at C. How you feel at C is mediated by your beliefs and thoughts at B; namely, that you will look an idiot in the eyes of others when you give your opinions. By keeping quiet at meetings, your anxiety-provoking thinking is relatively quiet and you remain 'safe'. We will return to the use of this model later in the chapter.

Tackling procrastination

When we ask individuals how they would feel if they got on with the task instead of avoiding it, they often reply 'great'. The next question is: why are they depriving themselves of this highly pleasurable feeling by avoiding the task? Anticipating feeling great does not mean that you have suddenly become motivated to carry out the task. There's a discomfort phase to get through which still acts as a deterrent to initiating the task; it's important to explore this discomfort phase in order to discover what holds you back, such as a feeling of being overwhelmed by the task; so you're reluctant to persevere with this unpleasant feeling until a positive one emerges of being in control.

The most obvious solution to procrastination might be an action plan (for example, time management schedule) in order to generate greater personal productivity; however, we would argue against this because, as we've already shown, procrastination is underpinned by emotional problems. You're not usually at your practical problem-solving best when you're emotionally upset, and 'relieving practical problems before emotional problems tends to rob clients of their motivation to solve their emotional problems, leaving them more comfortable yet still disturbed' (Grieger and Boyd, 1980: 36). Therefore, we usually suggest a two-pronged attack on procrastination: first tackle its emotional aspects before focusing on its practical aspects. The following coaching sessions with David will illustrate this.

Assessing the problem

DAVID: I'm missing deadlines at work with some of the projects I've been given to do. I can't seem to get motivated and therefore can't get started on them straight away. When I eventually get going it's all in an undisciplined rush driven by guilt.

MICHAEL: What are the consequences of missing deadlines?

DAVID: My boss gets pissed off and I keep on apologising to her with some pathetic excuse. I worry about what my colleagues think of me. I feel guilty about not meeting the deadlines and holding up my colleagues because I haven't done my work yet. I should be able to cut the mustard like most of my colleagues can.

MICHAEL: Are there any benefits from not getting on with it?

DAVID: Well, if I put these projects on the back burner then I can get on with something that's more enjoyable. It doesn't last long though because I start to worry again about missing the deadlines.

MICHAEL: Could you lose your job over your tardiness?

DAVID: I suppose I could but I assure you I don't want that to happen. I would love to be able to get going on these projects as soon as I'm given them. I want to stop messing about.

MICHAEL: Okay, let's take a closer look at this lack of motivation issue.

People who procrastinate often become emotionally upset about their inability to 'get on with it' or face up to the problem. These emotions (worry and guilt in the above example) are best viewed as secondary rather than as primary because they're a result of the procrastination, not the reason for it. The cognitive–emotive factors (that is, thoughts and feelings) that maintain procrastination are the main coaching focus. Much time can be wasted on discussing these secondary emotional problems thereby prolonging the person's procrastination in the coaching sessions (unless the client insists on some discussion of these issues). David was asked if he would be absorbed or distracted by these secondary problems in our quest to understand what drives his procrastination. He said no and was keen to find an answer to his avoidance behaviour.

I (MN) explained to David that procrastination often acts as a safety behaviour protecting the individual from an unpleasant or feared experience. However, the safety behaviour serves to maintain the underlying problem rather than solve it. Therefore, the 'way in' to understand the process of procrastination is to help the person reveal the unhelpful (that is, self- and task-defeating) ideas that maintain the problem.

Identifying these unhelpful ideas helps you to see how you're stopping yourself from task initiation or completion. This phase can be completed through a process known as inference chaining: the person's significant inferences about a situation are linked through a series of 'Let's assume . . . then what?' questions in order to uncover his core upset-producing thinking :

MICHAEL: Now close your eyes, David, and vividly imagine that you're starting on one of these avoided projects in an unmotivated and uninspired state. What specific project can you think of?

DAVID: Collating customer replies to one of our latest products.

MICHAEL: How are you feeling as you start the project?

DAVID: Apprehensive, irritable.

MICHAEL: You're feeling that way because . . .?

DAVID: Because it's boring and I have no interest in doing it . . . until I'm reluctantly forced into it by the looming deadline.

MICHAEL: Okay, but you're going to do it now rather than wait and be forced into it. What else is going through your mind?

DAVID: Why should I put myself through this when I don't have to yet?

MICHAEL: Let's assume you're putting yourself through it. Then what?

DAVID: *(becoming agitated)* I'm going to get even more angry. I'll probably chuck all the bloody paperwork into the waste bin. I shouldn't have to do things that are boring.

MICHAEL: Let's assume you are going to force yourself to do things that are boring. Then what?

DAVID: I'm going to get really fed up, bored stiff, angry, maybe rude to others. So why should I put myself through that experience?

MICHAEL: Okay, open your eyes. There seems to be two issues here: first, that you shouldn't have to do boring tasks when you're unmotivated or uninterested; secondly, if you do have to do them when you don't want to, you're going to get very upset about it. Would you agree with this analysis?

DAVID: Yes, I'd go along with it.

MICHAEL: Which of these two issues is more important to you: the lack of motivation or getting upset while carrying out these tasks?

DAVID: I don't follow what you mean.

MICHAEL: Well, if you were motivated to carry out these projects would you get upset about doing them?

DAVID: Probably not, but I really can't see myself becoming that motivated about them. These projects are pretty boring.

MICHAEL: Okay, what about if you were able to get on with these boring projects straightaway without being motivated but able to tolerate or, more importantly, really tone down your anger?

DAVID: Hmm. I like the sound of that *(laughs)*. How do I do it then? I get embarrassed that at my age I'm still throwing the toys out of the pram!

MICHAEL: Well, what's the worst thing that will happen to you if you remain somewhat bad-tempered while working on one of your projects?

DAVID: Er . . . what's the worst thing? . . . just putting up with it I suppose until it wears off.

MICHAEL: Will it be the end of your world or will you never be happy again if you have to tolerate these feelings until they wear off?

DAVID: Of course not. It's learning to put up with them.

MICHAEL: What's even more important, as I've said, is to get rid of your anger – or reduce it to a mild irritability – as it interferes greatly with your work: you make more mistakes, produce poorer work and prolong the task.

DAVID: *(laughs)* I'll second that!

David was taught the cognitive–behavioural coaching viewpoint that our beliefs and attitudes about events rather than the events themselves largely create our emotional upsets and counterproductive behaviours. The ABC model of emotional problems was drawn on a whiteboard to show the task-blocking beliefs that maintained David's procrastination:

A 1 – Undertaking a boring task when unmotivated
B 1 – 'I shouldn't have to do what I don't want to do!'
C 1 – Irritability
A 2 – David notices how irritable he is
B 2 – 'I shouldn't have to feel like this and I can't stand it!'
C 2 – Anger about feeling irritable

Whether David starts the project or avoids it depends on whether the intensely unpleasant feelings at C2 are greater than at C1. As they are, David's behaviour is motivated by the avoidance of feeling angry. However, as the deadline comes ever closer, David's fear of missing it propels him into hasty action. Until that time comes, David avoids the anger associated with undertaking the project. In discussing this model with

David, he disclosed that in certain areas of his life (not just at work) he exhibited what we came to pinpoint as low frustration tolerance (LFT): 'If I'm going to feel pretty unpleasant about some task or activity, then I do my best to avoid doing it or put it off as long as possible because I can't stand feeling that way.' The antidote to LFT is to strive for higher frustration tolerance (HFT) by internalising a coping attitude to emotional upsets, setbacks and discomfort in life (for example, 'I don't like experiencing these unpleasant feelings but I can learn to tolerate them as it will help me to achieve my goals').

MICHAEL: What kind of attitude do you need to develop if you want to get to grips with this problem?

DAVID: Something like 'Stop moaning about how I feel and get on with it'. I want to be more disciplined and get it firmly fixed up here (tapping his head) that you can't avoid the boring stuff in your job.

MICHAEL: Or life. How will this new attitude help you?

DAVID: So I can meet my deadlines, not leave it to the last minute when it all becomes an undisciplined rush, as I've said before.

MICHAEL: So what will be the first step then?

DAVID: Well, I'm not starting a project tomorrow – I'm not that keen yet despite what I've just said. Let's take it a little easier to start with.

MICHAEL: Okay, are there any things at home that you avoid for the same reasons?

DAVID: Yes. DIY tasks that my wife keeps on about and some social occasions I put off because they'll bore me.

MICHAEL: How about carrying out a few of these tasks in order to prove to yourself . . .?

DAVID: I won't like doing them because of the way I'm going to feel but that is no reason for me to avoid doing them. Yes, I'll do a few.

MICHAEL: And remember, you can change how you feel about doing these tasks. You don't have to see yourself doing them forever in an angry state.

The course of coaching

These and other tasks that David agreed to carry out are often called 'stay-in-there' assignments and consist of 'staying in rather than avoiding an aversive situation in order to work through the disturbed ideas and feelings about it' (Grieger and Boyd, 1980:156). Stay-in-there tasks can be carried out using prolonged exposure (giving yourself a big dose of discomfort) or brief exposure (smaller doses) until you're no longer upset about these situations.

Imagery exercises were introduced to promote constructive change (DiMattia and IJzermans, 2011). David was asked to imagine feeling extremely angry while carrying out a usually avoided task and then, while staying with the same task, to reduce his anger so he now only felt irritable. This emotional shift was achieved by cognitive change: from 'I can't stand feeling like this' to 'I can stand feeling like this without liking it in order to finish this project'. By practising this imagery technique several times daily for a couple of weeks, David was able to eventually feel only mild irritation when contemplating or carrying out boring tasks. Nothing terrible happened to him while doing these tasks, as the anticipation is usually worse than the actuality.

David also agreed to carry out a survey among his work colleagues on their attitudes towards undertaking boring tasks. He discovered that those who met their deadlines had a 'It's got to be done whether I like it or not' attitude while those, like himself, who procrastinated had LFT attitudes: 'I can't be bothered to do it unless someone puts a gun to my head' said one of his colleagues. As David tackled his workplace tasks, he said he saw himself moving out of the 'LFT camp' and towards the 'get on with it lot'. Reading a book on developing self-discipline helped him to accelerate this movement (Dryden, 2009).

He directed his mind to tackling the avoided workplace projects and was now able to absorb practical problem-solving tips as he was no longer angry. Some examples: he left a message on his desk that could not escape his eye, 'I have committed myself to getting rid of my procrastination – there will be no more excuses!' He divided his work into three categories: pending (no immediate action required); paramount (immediate action required) and projects (time to be allotted every day to these in order to meet deadlines). David was encouraged to keep a daily time log and note down every thirty minutes what he had done in that time. The purpose of the time log was to discover how he spent and, more importantly, how he wasted his time, for example, long phone calls, too much chit-chat with some colleagues, handling paperwork several times without doing anything constructive with it, allowing frequent interruptions in order to 'distract myself from my dull endeavours'. Through such tasks, David's time-wasting activities reduced considerably and his level of self-discipline increased significantly. David was now able to manage his time and himself more effectively in the service of his goals (for a detailed discussion of time management, see Chapter 4).

During the course of coaching, David sometimes continued to pro-crastinate over task completion, so a system of self-reinforcement was used. This involved rewards and penalties. David rewarded himself with such pleasures as an excellent claret in the evening for carrying out usu-ally avoided tasks while he penalised himself with extra DIY chores at home when he 'slid back' at work. After eight sessions David was ready to terminate coaching:

MICHAEL: Do you want to sum up what you've learnt about tackling your procrastination?

DAVID: Well, it seems so obvious in retrospect. I can carry out a task which is unpleasant or boring whether I'm motivated or not. Action is more important than motivation. I now meet my deadlines despite the fact that some of the projects I'm assigned are still as dull as ditch water.

MICHAEL: I'm happy to hear you're meeting your deadlines. What about the crucial problem of how upset you got, often very angry, when you had to do something that was highly boring?

DAVID: That was the real killer, or so it seemed at the time. I used to be very apprehensive about experiencing that feeling, so as soon as I got worked up and convinced myself that I couldn't stand feeling that way – good old LFT – then I threw in the towel. Now I've learnt how to put up with it, the anger seems to have gone because I now tell myself something very different.

MICHAEL: Which is . . .?

DAVID: Well, if tasks are boring or unpleasant, so what? Get on and do them. I still get flashes of anger sometimes though.

MICHAEL: That's to be expected as progress does not occur in a smooth, straight line. Obviously it's not just putting up with boring or unpleasant things for their own sake, but if doing so helps you to achieve your goals.

DAVID: Oh, I do understand that. I've been trying to convey that mes-sage to some of my colleagues who miss their deadlines for the same reasons I used to.

MICHAEL: Any luck?

DAVID: Not yet.

MICHAEL: But you've got the message loud and clear, I trust.

DAVID: Definitely.

Follow-up sessions were arranged for three, six and twelve months' after our last session to determine if David had maintained his gains from coaching. David could contact me if he encountered serious problems within this time period and could not solve them on his own.

Conclusion

To change a behaviour pattern like procrastination requires you to do much more of what you've been avoiding – work! (Knaus, 2010). This involves uncovering and then disputing forcefully those self-defeating thoughts and beliefs which insist that a task or situation is, for whatever reason, too difficult to face. By developing an anti-procrastination attitude, what appears to be unbearable eventually becomes bearable as action replaces inaction and avoidance.

Chapter 4

Time management

Introduction

Time is endless, but your time is limited. Do you use it to your best advantage? Expressions such as 'There are not enough hours in the day', 'Where does the time go?' and 'I've got too much time on my hands' suggest not. These expressions indicate you're not in control of time, for example, you're in a constant state of hurry as you race through the tasks on your ever lengthening to-do lists, or you're drifting through life without clearly defined values or goals to guide you. On the other hand, you may know individuals who pack a lot of productive activity into each day and wonder: 'How can they do it and I can't?' Time is neutral, though: it does not tick faster on a busy day any more than it ticks slower on a boring or listless day, or favours one person over another. As with the other topics in this book, time management is really about self-management: time itself doesn't have to be managed as it proceeds one second at a time all on its own! In other words, in order to understand why you don't make the best use of your time, look to yourself and not to the clock.

People who consult us for a coaching programme often tell us that their diaries are distressingly full, nothing can be cut out and everything is equally important. We know from our own personal and coaching experiences that this perceived helplessness is not the case but why can't they see it?

Poor time management

Davis *et al.* (1995) list some indicators of poor time management:

- Constant rushing, for example between meetings or tasks.
- Frequent lateness, for example attending meetings, seeing clients or meeting deadlines.

- Low productivity, energy and motivation, for example, 'I can't seem to get worked up about anything apart from pay day.'
- Frustration, for example, 'I always seem to be at the beck and call of others.'
- Impatience, for example, 'Where the hell is that information I asked him for? He's holding me back from getting on with my work.'
- Chronic vacillation between alternatives, for example, 'I've been scratching my head for weeks over this. Whatever option I choose is going to put me at a big disadvantage. I don't know which way to jump.'
- Difficulty setting and achieving goals, for example, 'I'm not sure what my role is or what is expected of me.'
- Procrastination, that is, continually putting off starting a task or activity.

To this list could be added inter alia:

- Perfectionism, that is, the uncompromising pursuit of exceptionally high standards, for example, 'I will only accept one hundred per cent achievement; anything less is a failure.' This may mean you spend too long on tasks to get them 'just right', go very slowly to avoid making any mistakes or try to avoid the task because you fear doing a less-than-perfect job. Perfectionism is often a cause of procrastination.
- Getting bogged down in details, that is, you cannot grasp the main issues because of your over-attention to details: 'I can't help being a dot the i's and cross the t's type of person.'
- Feeling overwhelmed by your workload, for example, 'Now I understand what being stressed-out really means!'
- Unassertiveness – not standing up for yourself, for example, 'I don't like arguments, so even though it's not my job, I'll do it to keep the peace.'
- Little delegation of work, for example, 'If you want a job done properly, then do it yourself.'

Jason was always racing from task to task whether at home or work; to others, he seemed to have a busy and enviably full life. Jason, in contrast, felt he was just 'rushing around like a headless chicken – I do a lot but don't seem to achieve much or value what I do'. If he stopped rushing everywhere, stood still and took stock of his life, what would he do differently? 'Haven't a clue,' he replied. Pauline worked in a job that provided little stimulation or stretched her capabilities (she was in danger of 'rustout' rather than burnout). When I (MN) asked her what kind of work she would like to fill her time with she said, 'I don't really know.' These replies demonstrate that time was being wasted or mismanaged because both Jason and Pauline had no real sense of purpose or direction in their lives. The essence of time management is knowing what your values and goals are in life and making the optimum use of your time to achieve these ends.

Knowing what your goals and values are doesn't mean that time will automatically subordinate itself to your new-found sense of purpose, however. You will need to review how you use your time and phase out those activities that are not goal-directed. This process requires adopting new attitudes and behaviours and tackling those obstacles to change (for example, unassertiveness, perfectionism) in order to make time management a daily and lifetime reality rather than an intriguing but elusive concept.

Making clear what your values and goals are

Values help you to determine what's important in your life. As Sichel observes:

> They are the silent forces behind many of your actions and decisions. The goal of 'values clarification' is for their influence to become fully conscious, for you to explore and honestly acknowledge what you truly value at this time in your life. You can be more self-directed and effective when you know which values you really choose to keep and live by as an adult, and which ones will get priority over others.
>
> (1993, section III: 48)

Some important values may include: financial security, doing well in one's career, high standards, loving relationships, good friends, keeping fit, treating people fairly, fighting injustice, family life, making the most of every day, visiting interesting places, working hard. If you have difficulty identifying your important values, Hauck (1988) suggests the following exercise: imagine yourself on your deathbed reflecting on a full and happy life. What were the ingredients that made it so? You don't want to reach old age full of 'if only . . .' regrets about what you didn't do or have, just as the poet John Betjeman, for example, lamented not having enough sex in his life. Another exercise is to imagine that you have a terminal illness and you will be dead in six months' time. What activities would fill these remaining months of your life?

Exercises such as these can help you to focus on what may be missing from your life or what, though appearing to be important, is, in fact, easily given up. Be careful when doing a values clarification exercise as you may push yourself to endorse values that aren't important to you but you think should be such as reading philosophy books to create the impression of a 'deep thinker' (why you need to create this impression needs investigation). When you have identified your priorities (for example, physical fitness), these need to be translated into goals. A useful acronym to guide goal selection is SMART:

S – Specific: for example, 'I want to be physically fitter in three months' time.'

M – Measurable: what is your present level of fitness? What outcomes would you be looking for in three months' time? What progress markers would tell you that you're on course for goal success?

A – Achievable: is there a reasonable expectation that your goal can be attained? Do you have the resources to join a gym or the ability to devise your own fitness programme?

R – Realistic: are you really committed to this fitness programme given the fact you're not giving up cigarettes, reducing your alcohol intake or monitoring your diet?

T – Timebound: can your goal be realised within the allotted time? Are you taking into account your other responsibilities and activities?

The above example relates to a short-term goal of three months; when this is attained, you can decide if you want to maintain that level of fitness or set yourself tougher physical fitness goals. While it's understandable that you will get excited about the prospect of achieving your goals, remember this: 'People who visualize themselves taking the practical steps needed to achieve their goals are far more likely to succeed than those who simply fantasize about their dreams becoming a reality' (Wiseman, 2009: 328–9). We would add that visualising the practical steps should also include troubleshooting possible blocks to goal progress. Wiseman also suggests that people are more likely to keep to their promises if they go public (to family, friends, colleagues) about their goals than if they keep them private: 'It seems that although keeping your aims to yourself helps ease the fear of failure, it also makes it too easy to avoid changing your life and drift back into old habits and routines' (2009: 91).

As we've said, ensure that your goals are in line with your values, so if you value highly family life then your goal would be to arrive home at a reasonable time every day – unless a crisis supervenes – to spend more time with your children before their bedtime. Also, your goals should reflect the presence of something you desire (for example, 'I want to finish this essay in one month') rather than the absence of something undesirable (for example, 'I don't want to keep on procrastinating over finishing this bloody essay!').

On a different note, many writers have pointed out that endless goal-achievement can become oppressive: you feel a sense of emptiness or anxiety if you haven't lined up your next target. In order to deal with these feelings, also focus on goals that don't have an end point (unlike SMART goals) but are, instead, an intrinsic part of an enjoyable and meaningful life – therefore you're not worrying about what to do next. For me (MN) reading, long walks and films (particularly of the 1960s) are lifelong passions, and for me (WD) these passions are daily exercise, writing commitments and helping clients to deal with their difficulties in order to improve the quality of their life. These activities transcend the necessary goals we set ourselves to maintain our businesses as coaches and therapists.

Monitoring your time

Having established what your values and goals are, the next step is to discover how you actually spend your time. This is achieved through the use of a time log (see Figure 4.1). The best way to fill in a time log is to record each activity and the time taken to complete it *as it occurs*. A contemporaneous account of time spent will obviously be more accurate than a retrospective one. If this proves too difficult to do, then try to ensure that you record each hour's activities at the end of it. The time recorded in your log should equal the amount of time spent at work (if not, then maybe you're not being diligent enough in filling in your log or something unusual occurred which you didn't consider to be part of your daily work routine and therefore omitted it). If you leave filling in your time log until you get home from work, it's likely you will produce a distorted account of your working day (for example, 'How long did that phone call take? I can't remember. I'll put down twenty minutes to be on the safe side').

A time log can cover every waking moment of each day (rather than just time spent at work) as you may want to undertake a time management review of every aspect of your life. Keeping a time log for one or two days will probably provide insufficient information for a thorough review of

Date	Time	Activity
	9.00	
	10.00	
	11.00	
	12.00	
	13.00	
	14.00	
	15.00	
	16.00	
	17.00	
	18.00	
	19.00	

Figure 4.1 Example of a time log.

your time as you may not spot behavioural patterns emerging (for example, procrastination, unassertiveness) or how often certain individuals encroach on your time. Keeping a time log will increase your workload in the short term but enable you to see where changes can be made in order for longer-term benefits to be gained. Of course, you may know already what your time wasters are and therefore don't need to keep a time log, but you may still be unsure why you keep wasting time and want to find out.

Determining task priority

To discover this, you can prioritise your activities in terms of their urgency and importance (Covey, 1989). Activities can be placed in four categories:

1. Urgent and important
2. Not urgent but important
3. Urgent but not important
4. Not urgent and not important

Category 1 activities include responding to crises and rushing to meet looming deadlines. If you spend too much of your time responding to immediate events you may be moving into the danger zone of high stress levels and possible burnout. As Fontana observes:

> People who in their professional lives seem always to be at the mercy of circumstances are usually those who wait for things to happen, and then *react* to them. People who seem more on top of things are usually those who see things coming, and *act* in good time to guard against them (or benefit from them).
>
> (1989: 59–60; emphases in original)

Category 2 activities encourage thinking ahead (for example, 'What steps do I need to take now to meet my performance targets in six months' time?') instead of being glad just to have survived the day at the office – taking preventative measures to reduce the frequency of crises and problems, and developing balance in your life. Remember not to neglect these activities just because they're not urgent, otherwise they soon will be (for example, you become run-down through overwork because you kept putting off implementing a 'less time at work and more fun and exercise' plan). Jones suggests that you should 'aim to schedule 60 per cent of your time for proactive tasks, leaving the other 40 per cent available for reactive and maintenance tasks [that is, keeping things running smoothly], as well as unexpected interruptions, which may occur anyway' (1998: 49).

Category 3 activities often include responding to the requests of others (for example, 'I need your help to finish my report by Thursday'; 'Listen, can you chair that meeting for me, I'm so busy?'). As for category 1, you're reacting to events but these activities aren't important in helping to achieve your key personal and organisational goals.

Category 4 activities involve looking busy, for example, shuffling papers, hurrying to and fro, organising your desk, repeatedly checking and reading your emails without dealing with them. You may convince yourself that endlessly revising your time management plan is an important activity when, in fact, it's time-wasting. Activities in this category are neither urgent nor important and should be removed from your daily schedule.

As indicated above, the majority of your time should be devoted to important (that is, goal-directed) but not urgent activities (category 2). This emphasis on what is important to *you* may smack of selfishness, but we would suggest it's more accurately called enlightened self-interest, that is, you put your own interests and goals first most of the time while putting those of others, particularly significant others, a close second. If

you feel directionless or overburdened and your desires remain unful-
filled, what kind of person might you be at home and work? Being at your
best is more likely to bring out the best in others.

Pinpointing emotional blocks to change

Using a time management plan to implement your priorities in life might
seem relatively straightforward – but what often prevents or delays
implementation are emotional difficulties. For example, you feel guilty
because you want to spend more time on your own interests and you
believe your children will suffer as a result ('and that will prove what
a bad parent I am'); you make yourself anxious about the prospect of
saying no to a colleague's request for you to take on some of his work
because this will incur his disapproval ('He'll think I'm uncooperative
and start gossip about me. I don't want that'); or you have a low threshold
for tolerating boring or unpleasant but important activities and become
angry when you have to do them ('Watching paint dry would be more
interesting than trying to make sense of these damn figures!'). People
who have read books or attended seminars and workshops on time management often fail to act on what they've learnt because identifying and
resolving emotional blocks was not part of the content. Therefore, a time
management programme should ideally include an emotional management component.

Becoming better organised

This is achieved through the use of to-do lists with each task prioritised
and given a deadline: for example, your first task is your top priority
(due 20 July); second is medium priority (mid-August approx.); and is
low priority (no deadline). Remove time-wasting activities from your
schedule as they add nothing of value to your work (for example, too
many tea-breaks, office gossip, phone calls to friends). If you have several top-priority tasks vying for your attention, do the most unpleasant
or difficult one first; too many top-priority tasks means you're not dis-
criminating enough between what's essential for completion today and
what can wait; and finish one task before starting another, otherwise you
might find yourself flitting between several tasks and doing each one
suboptimally.

Obviously not all top-priority activities can be finished in one fell
swoop because, for example, you need further information which will
not be forthcoming for several days. When this information becomes

available, then the unfinished task becomes a top priority for that day. If a task is big or complicated, then break it down into smaller sections and assign an allotted period of time to each section (it's usually better to overestimate the time it will take rather than underestimate it). Sometimes a confusion can arise between time management and task management (Northedge, 1990): if you concentrate on time then you may overvalue the hours you've 'clocked up' rather than what you've actually achieved (you may have spent two hours on a project but the productive portion was the first hour); on the other hand, if you overly focus on the task, you may let it go on for too long ('I've got to get it finished. To hell with the time!'). Obviously a balance is required between time and task management in order not to waste valuable time or engage in unproductive work.

A common problem with to-do lists is overloading of tasks:

> We make daily to-do lists that couldn't be accomplished even if there were no interruptions during the day, which there always are. By the time the weekend arrives, there are more unfinished tasks than ever, but we keep deferring them and expecting to get through them with miraculous speed. That's why, as productivity experts have found, an executive's daily to-do list for Monday often contains more work than could be done [in] the entire week (Baumeister and Tierney, 2012: 63).

In the light of these comments, when you're thinking about your to-do lists focus on removing items instead of adding them, so the actual list doesn't seem daunting. If you don't like the idea of to-do lists, Baumeister and Tierney (2012: 249) suggest a 'to-don't list: a catalog of things that you *don't* have to worry about once you write them down' (emphasis in original). So you can relax for the time being but action plans will still be required for task completion.

Prime performance in prime time

To produce high-quality work, Mann advises you find out when you work best: 'Some people are "owls", who work best in the evening; others are "larks" who are at their most alert in the morning. Do the most important and demanding jobs when you are normally at your best' (1998: 144). Quick et al. (2013) call this working at your best internal prime time. Adair suggests that the majority of us are larks and 'any task requiring solitude, concentration and creative thinking is best done before 10.00 a.m. You can accomplish more with less effort if you programme important items at this high performance time' (1988: 68). Internal prime time requires uninterrupted time: 'A clear couple of hours when you can mount an all-out attack on a problem is worth two days full of interruptions' (Atkinson, 1994: 68). Therefore, let others know you don't wish to be disturbed, shut your door and put your telephone on silent. If you work in an open-plan office, then you will have to 'withdraw' into your work space and create an imaginary wall around you and deal assertively with people who breach it for gossip, chit-chat or impatiently want their questions answered now! Some companies allow employees to use an indicator system (for example, small flag on the desk) that reminds others not to interrupt.

Is it working?

If your new time management system is working effectively then you should notice some of the following improvements: increased energy, productivity and motivation, greater sense of control, more decisive, proactive rather than reactive, not taking problems home, acting assertively, tackling procrastination and perfectionism, improved timekeeping. Above all, there should now be enough hours in the day to complete your most important activities.

Coaching example

Richard was a thirty-year-old married man with three children. He described his day at the office as 'keeping my nose to the grindstone. I don't seem to have time to think. Everything comes at me and I just get caught up in it.' He was unhappy with his style of work; home and social life were affected by his tiredness and irritability. He admired work colleagues who controlled their day in a way that he was unable to: 'They enjoy their life both in and out of the office.' When I (MN) asked Richard what he valued in his life, he listed five key items:

1. Doing a good job
2. Family life
3. Being fit
4. More time for social activities
5. Being seen as likeable and helpful

The next stage was to translate his values into specific goals. He said if he could 'crack the work problem then the other things [2, 3 and 4] would fall into place'. He said his goal was to 'manage things better at work'. This was an aim rather than a concrete goal, however:

MICHAEL: What specific things would you need to achieve in order to realise your aim of managing things better at work?

RICHARD: Well for starters, meetings ending on time, keeping phone calls to the point, saying no to colleagues when they dump tasks on me which are not really within my remit, and keeping interruptions brief and fewer so I can spend more time on the really important tasks.

MICHAEL: Okay. Let's see how you currently spend your time.

Richard's time log

Richard kept a daily time log for the next few weeks so we could get a clear pattern of his behaviour (see Figure 4.2.).

Studying his time log, we note that if Richard did it today instead of in 2000 (for the first edition of this book), it would no doubt include endlessly checking and reading his emails without doing anything with them; roaming the Internet and visiting social networking sites (unless your company has blocked access to them); playing with iPhones, iPads and other electronic gadgets, but the time wasting would remain the same. In analysing Richard's time log, it was obvious that some of his activities were incompatible with his goals such as meetings overrunning, spending too long on the phone, tolerating frequent interruptions. What lay behind his difficulty, for example, in finishing meetings on time as he had overall control as the chairman?

RICHARD: I suppose I need to be more forceful with getting some people to stick to the agenda and not ramble on.

MICHAEL: But what prevents you from doing that?

RICHARD: I'm not really sure. I suppose I want people to leave the meeting feeling good.

MICHAEL: But how would you feel if you interrupted someone and asked them to stick to the agenda?

RICHARD: I'd be anxious about doing that?

MICHAEL: Because . . .?

RICHARD: Because they might not like it.

MICHAEL: And if they didn't like it . . .?

RICHARD: Then they won't like me. I know it's pathetic but there it is: I like to be liked.

MICHAEL: Okay, it's nice to be liked, but at the expense of sabotaging your goals?

RICHARD: Well, I don't want to become an obnoxious bastard.

Date: 6. 6. 2000	Time	Activity	
	9.00	Telephone calls	(20 mins)
		Correspondence	(15 mins)
		Interruption	(15 mins)
		Telephone call	(10 mins)
	10.00	Meeting	(90 mins)
	11.00	Meeting contd.	
		Paperwork	(15 mins)
		Tea break	(5 mins)
		Fed up	(10 mins)
	12.00	Project	(15 mins)
		Phone call	(10 mins)
		Project	(20 mins)
		Interruption	(15 mins)
	13.00	Lunch (rushed)	(15 mins)
		Listening to colleague's problems	(20 mins)
		Urgent call from customer	(15 mins)
		Helping colleague with paperwork	(10 mins)
	14.00	Meeting	(75 mins)
	15.00	Meeting contd.	
		Writing report	(10 mins)
		Interruption	(5 mins)
		Fed up	(15 mins)
		Writing report	(10 mins)
		Phone call	(15 mins)
	16.00	Phone call contd.	
		Tea break	(5 mins)
		Writing report	(20 mins)
		Fed up	(10 mins)
		Interruptions	(15 mins)
	17.00	Writing report	(5 mins)
		Fed up	(5 mins)
		Phone call	(10 mins)
		Tidying desk	(5 mins)
		Staring out of the window	(5 mins)
		Trying to look busy	(30 mins)
		as manager still on premises	
	18.00	Going home	

Figure 4.2 A sample day from Richard's time log.

MICHAEL: There are more alternatives available than just nice or obnoxious bastard. Let's just say you politely interrupted a verbose colleague (Richard mentions a name), and he ticked you off for being
rude, what choices do you have at that point?

RICHARD: I can agree or disagree with him.

MICHAEL: How would you vote at the present time?

RICHARD: I would agree with him and that would make me unlikeable in
his eyes and my own.

MICHAEL: Do you know if he likes you in the first place?

RICHARD: I didn't think about that. I just assumed he would because I try
to be nice to everyone.

MICHAEL: Another point: are you allowing him to define you as likeable or unlikeable instead of you making up your own mind about
yourself?

RICHARD: I suppose I am doing that. I never thought about it in that way
before. From that perspective, I am whatever people see me as, a
kind of slave really.

MICHAEL: But a slave who can find a way to free himself.

RICHARD: Easier said than done.

MICHAEL: True, but, in essence, not being liked by some people is only
a big deal if you make it one. Give up going to work with a 'please
like me' attitude and you will be able to claw back the time you are
currently wasting.

Richard realised other time-wasting activities were linked to his need
(he admitted it was much stronger than a want) to be liked, for example,
delegating little work in case some of his subordinates resented it, staying late at the office to impress his boss and catch up with his own
work, being a 'friendly ear' for others' problems. To combat his need to
be liked, Richard's action plan was to internalise a philosophy of self-
acceptance, that is, to forcefully and persistently accept himself irrespective of how others saw him ('I don't want to become insensitive or
selfish, but I will start saying no when justified and if others get funny
about it, so be it').

Some examples of his new outlook: with colleagues who frequently
interrupted him, he pointed to the 'Do Not Disturb' sign on his door
and suggested a later time when he would not be so busy – he didn't
break off from his work while conveying this information. While chair-
ing meetings he emphasised how important it was to keep comments
concise and pertinent to the agenda and 'verbiage was a waste of everybody's time as we all have busy departments to get back to'; meetings

now took half their usual time and unnecessary ones were purged from his daily schedule. Phone calls were also kept brief and to the point. He no longer allowed others to dump their work on him; instead he would advise them how to do it or tell them it was their responsibility to carry out the task. He delegated much more of his work so 'I can focus on the essentials'.

Richard's bouts of procrastination over difficult or boring tasks were tackled by developing a forceful motivational statement: 'Getting the task finished is more important than whether it's pleasant or not, so get on with it!' Time spent on paperwork was reduced by only handling it once (OHIO): every time he picked up a piece of paper he put a tick in the corner; more than one tick on the paper meant Richard was returning to it without making any decisions about it. His 'fed up' periods virtually vanished from his daily schedule ('That's because I feel I'm more in control rather than being or letting myself be controlled by events or others').

Richard said he got strange looks from some colleagues and when they asked him if 'I was alright, I told them the reasons for my new behaviour. Some of them have been supportive, others less so but they were the ones I used to let take advantage of me.' With more time now released, Richard was able to prioritise his day, focusing mainly on important tasks. He made sure he took an unhurried lunch break on most days and went to the local gym three times a week. He got home earlier in a better frame of mind and was able to enjoy domestic and social life without the overlay of work worries:

RICHARD: When I go to work now I really am focused on it, the work. Being my new self, so to speak, rather than needing to be liked has really cleared a path through my life. Decisions I now make are based on the priorities of the job, not on my emotional priorities.

MICHAEL: Is self-acceptance now an important value for you?

RICHARD: Very much so. In fact, there are a couple of people at work who I now recognise as fellow sufferers and their time management skills are as bad as mine were. So I might have a word with them and see if they're interested in learning what I did.

MICHAEL: Good. Spread the word to the receptive.

Conclusion

Effective time management doesn't mean that every second of your day has to be accounted for, but that much of your time is directed towards achieving your goals. Like any other change, you will need to monitor your time management skills on a daily basis to prevent returning to poor use of your time (in Richard's case, time mismanagement might indicate he has slipped back to his approval needs). As the time management literature continually reminds us, time is a precious resource and each second, minute, hour that ticks by can never be replaced. Therefore, use it wisely.

Chapter 5

Persistence

Introduction

Writing a chapter on persistence requires persistence on our part. After all, what is there to say apart from that if you want to bring about change in your life then persist until this change is achieved? In considering the nature of persistence, there are more factors involved than simply urging yourself to 'keep at it' and 'don't give up' or being reassured by others that 'persistence pays off' (for example, what prevents you from being persistent in particular contexts?). Persistence requires the development of a philosophy of endurance, not just for today or next week, but for the long term. Some dictionary definitions of persistence include 'continuing obstinately' which implies behavioural inflexibility or unthinkingly pushing forward. We leave obstinacy out of our discussion of persistence because we want you to think and act flexibly in the face of changing circumstances as you strive to reach your goals.

Also, not all persistence is admirable or worthwhile – pointless persistence. For example, a person may proclaim 'I'm not a quitter', conveying a dogged, heroic determination to always prevail no matter what; yet his present persistence to save his clearly failing business by pumping large amounts of money into it has amassed very large, unsustainable debts. The advice from business friends and consultants is to 'throw in the towel' but he can't see past his own ego, thinks they're all wrong and if he keeps on reminding himself he is a fighter not a quitter – which is the only consolation he has left – he will come through with a triumphant 'I told you so!' Unfortunately, the outcome is financial ruin and fractured relationships. So, was it worth it? 'I gave it my best shot; what else could I do? Anyway, onwards and upwards.' This individual is likely to repeat such experiences as he looks outwards ('It just wasn't to be this time, that's all') rather than inwards to explain what happened.

One of the essential qualities for success and achievement in life is persistence. Yet we often want change without working at it – we like the idea of change rather than the actual struggle to bring it about. Why does a New Year's Eve resolution become New Year's Day irresolution? How many times have you wanted to stop smoking, lose weight, get fitter, make a career change, leave a dull relationship, or even take a trip up the Amazon? What stopped you from doing it? We would suggest it was partly the effort and upheaval in your life that this might involve. Even if you say you're motivated to change, this doesn't mean that change will inevitably occur. Motivation consists of three components (Arnold *et al.*, 1995):

1. Direction – what you're trying to do or achieve
2. Effort – how hard you're trying
3. Persistence – how long you continue trying.

You may know which direction you're going in, put in a lot of effort initially to get there, but give up your goal because you lack the persistence to sustain the effort to reach it. Grieger states that goal-directed behaviour is a '24-hour-a-day, 7-day-a-week thing' (1991: 60). You may blanch at this 'extreme' view of what change entails, but then you have to ask yourself what you mean by a commitment to change. Butler and Hope suggest that if you want to break what you consider to be a bad habit (for example, tranquilliser dependence, smoking, comfort eating) 'then this means becoming absolutely clear about whether you really do want to change. You will need to be motivated not only to break the habit, but in order to be able to persist' (2007: 353).

Some of the people we see in our coaching practice hedge their commitments to change with 'ifs', 'buts' and 'howevers' (a vocabulary of caution and unease), for example, 'I'm willing to put in the work if I can be sure I will succeed' and 'I do want to change but I'm worried about the hard work that lies ahead'. Thomas Edison famously remarked that 'genius is one per cent inspiration, ninety-nine per cent perspiration'. We take the light bulb for granted thanks to his 'perspiration'. Perspiration or sweat-soaked striving may not be an image of change that appeals to you; instead, you may look for a quick fix, an instant solution to your problems (and there's a large industry of dubious therapies and programmes all promising you great outcomes for little effort; such claims are made far ahead of the research evidence to support them). We sometimes ask people to calculate how much time they've wasted looking for quick and easy solutions and how much time it might have taken to actually tackle the problem. The usual answer is that the latter approach would probably have taken a fraction of the time consumed by the former, but even that admission doesn't stop the search for an instant solution.

Three key insights

In our coaching practice, we usually provide people with what we consider are three key insights into the development, maintenance and eventual improvement of their difficulties:

1. Upsetting ourselves is largely determined by our irrational (self-defeating) ideas. This observation has been pointed out by many writers and philosophers down the ages. To take one example: 'The meaning of things lies not in things themselves, but in our attitudes towards them' (Antoine de Saint-Exupéry, French writer and aviator). If you want to discover why you react in certain ways (for example, anxiously) to particular events (for example, meeting new people), focus on the meaning (attitudes) you bring to the things (events) rather than on the things themselves.
2. No matter how or when we acquired our irrational ideas, we remain upset in the present because we continually reindoctrinate or brainwash ourselves with these ideas and act in ways that strengthen them.
3. The only enduring way to overcome our emotional difficulties is through persistent hard work and practice – to think, feel and act against our irrational ideas.

When we discuss these insights with people and how they apply to their own difficulties, they often see the first two insights on the list as psychologically liberating because they now view their problems within their control rather than ascribing them to external factors that they can't change. However, the implications of the third seem less liberating because of the hard work required of them to translate theoretical understanding and remediation of their problems into daily practice. This translation involves the negotiation of self-help assignments to be carried out by the person between sessions in order to accelerate and deepen the process of change as well as put the person in the driving seat (that is, learning to become her own coach).

Trying or doing

When we ask people if they'll actually undertake these self-help tasks, a usual reply is 'I'll try' rather than 'I'll do it'. While this reply usually indicates that they will make an effort of some sort, it also denotes a lack of commitment on their part because they haven't yet grasped the philosophical implications of what real change actually requires from them – persistent and forceful action. They may have been trying for some considerable time to overcome a problem, but to no avail. So when they come to us for coaching, we ask them if they want to continue with the same attitude that's so far proved unproductive. If people don't carry out their agreed self-help assignments, we persist in finding the reasons for their non-compliance and seeking ways to overcome it.

We communicate to people the difference between trying and doing by asking them for example: 'When this session is finished, will you try to leave the room or will you do it? Did you try to get dressed this morning or did you do it?' Doing gets results but trying doesn't. If some people are still unclear about what we're driving at, we may offer them a book and ask them to try and take it. If someone takes it, we remind them the task was to try and take it, not take it. By this time, the point has usually sunk in and a 'doing' outlook starts to become part of their daily life (to emphasise this point, you may wish to add mentally the initial 'D' for 'doing' to your name, for example, Jane D. Brown). Next time you say 'I'll try' with regard to effecting desired changes in your life, consider if it will really galvanise you not only into action but also sustained action (you know what it usually means when your children say that they'll try to tidy their bedroom or do their school homework).

The meaning of willpower

Sometimes we're puzzled why people who declare that they possess willpower fail to achieve their goals . . . until we analyse their definitions of willpower. Often these revolve around the determination to change but stop there (for example, 'I'm determined to lose weight. It's just a matter of having willpower and then everything falls into place'). Willpower is easy to invoke but difficult to put into practice. Willpower (self-control) is directing your mind and behaviour to achieving your desired outcomes and restraining the impulses that interfere with this process. Such outcomes could be finishing this book within the publisher's deadline, training for and completing a marathon, staying out of debt, learning a language in order to speak it fluently or keeping to the recommended foods since your diagnosis of diabetes.

Pinker (2011: 598) observes that 'aside from intelligence, no other trait [self-control] augurs as well for a healthy and successful life' while Baumeister and Tierney (2012: 2) state 'that improving willpower is the

surest way to a better life'. Improving willpower starts with setting yourself a goal; outlining the action steps required to achieve it and having the
energy to execute those steps (don't deplete your energy on less important tasks so that you're tired, irritable or exhausted when starting your
more important goal-related tasks – you'll probably give up); monitoring
your progress towards the goal; overcoming any blocks along the way;
and reminding yourself regularly of the benefits of having willpower.
Each time you achieve your goal it strengthens your willpower as it
demonstrates you can implement your intentions. It's better to start with
moderately challenging goals to get the process going rather than beginning with unrealistic targets which will probably result in you giving up
making changes, for example, 'I'm going to run five miles every night'
when you've been a couch potato for twenty years! You won't be able to
develop unlimited willpower, so use your resources carefully and choose
your goals wisely. One final point. Self-control doesn't mean complete
self-denial, for example, you could decide to stick to one chocolate bis-
cuit with your cup of tea instead of your usual practice of wolfing down
six.

Failing to persist

In our experience, some of the following reasons may account for why
you either fail to persist in your goal-directed endeavours or sabotage
your efforts at doing so.

Short-range hedonism

This refers to seeking immediate satisfaction and pleasure at the expense
of your longer-term goals, for example, you spend more time at college
partying than studying and thereby fail to get the necessary grades for
admission to your university of choice. You act as if there's no future
for you to consider, an abstraction that will never materialise. In order to
reach your longer-term goals, you usually have to forgo some (but not
all) short-term pleasures but one of the hardest things for people to do is
to work towards their long-term goals while putting up with short-term
discomfort. Short-range hedonism usually involves wanting to avoid
pain, discomfort, inconvenience even though you know that this outlook
will block you from achieving an important goal (for example, 'I know
I should get myself into a rehab centre and sort out my alcohol problem
but it's just too much hassle at the present time'). Looking beyond short-
range hedonism requires 'exercising the faculty of reason [as] it goes

hand in hand with self-control . . . It is reason – a deduction of the long-term consequences of an action – that gives the self reasons to control the self' (Pinker, 2011: 645).

'If only I knew how it started'

People often convince themselves that if they discover the causes of their problems (usually lying somewhere in the past), then they will be motivated to overcome them or they will be spontaneously cured of them. Believing that the solution to your problems lies in the past rather than in the present is what Grieger and Boyd (1980) call the 'past history trap'. Past events continue to have an undesirable effect upon you today because of your *current* thinking about these events (for example, 'I still see myself as second best because my parents favoured my older sister over me'), so it's your current thinking that you need to work on so that tomorrow can be a little better than today.

'How can I persist if i'm no good?'

You may want to tackle an addiction problem, for example, but you consider yourself to be worthless for having the addiction. With this self-image of worthlessness, you assume that attempts at change will be futile because you can only see the bad in yourself rather than the good that may come from your persistence. We would focus on teaching you self-acceptance (that is, not judging yourself in any way, only your actions, for example, 'What I did was bad which caused havoc in my life and I want to learn how not to repeat such behaviour, but I'm not bad for doing what I did'), so that your persistence at overcoming the addiction is not undermined or continually called into question by your self-depreciation.

'I'm not me any more'

This apparent loss of identity can halt the process of change in its tracks. Giving up familiar but self-defeating thoughts and behaviours can feel strange or unnatural as you work towards acquiring a more productive problem-solving outlook. This dissonant state created by the clash or tension between the new, emerging self and the old, 'clinging' self can lead you to give up trying to change in order to feel 'natural again'. These concerns are illustrated in this extract from a coaching transcript:

SANDRA: It feels very strange not reacting as much as I used to, you know, lashing out when people criticised me. I'm glad of course but that doesn't lessen the strangeness of it all.

MICHAEL: What's strange about it?

SANDRA: Well, it probably sounds silly to you but that lashing out, being defensive or whatever you want to call it, was part of me, my sense of who I was. I feel I've lost part of myself.

MICHAEL: Do you think you've defined yourself too narrowly on the basis of a particular behaviour you engage in?

SANDRA: Maybe. I can certainly see and have experienced the benefits of keeping cool when people criticise me. I like feeling more in control of myself.

MICHAEL: Aren't you still Sandra but with some welcome changes?

SANDRA: I suppose so.

MICHAEL: How do you think you will see yourself in six months' time if you persist with these changes?

SANDRA: I suppose these changes will feel more natural, part of me.

MICHAEL: And how will you view the old, lashing out behaviour?

SANDRA: I suppose that will seem rather strange and distant. I might even have trouble remembering I behaved like that.

MICHAEL: So what will you need to do if you want to make these changes natural and permanent?

SANDRA: Tolerate these strange feelings and see them as part of the change process. If I see it that way, then these feelings probably won't last for too long.

MICHAEL: Exactly. That's the way it usually works. Remember this rule of thumb about change: 'If you ain't feeling strange, then you ain't experiencing change!'

'Others must help me'

Your efforts at change are based on demanding the support of others (for example, 'If I give up smoking, then so must you. I can't hope to stop with you sitting there puffing away'). You put the responsibility for your change on to others (for example, partner, parents) as well as blame them if you're unsuccessful (for example, 'I told you I couldn't stop smoking if you too don't give up'). Demanding that others must 'hold your hand' will dilute your personal responsibility for change and reinforce your beliefs that you're too fragile to go it alone or stick at it.

'I was born this way – I can't change'

This view that you can't change and it's hopeless to try is based on a confusion between predisposition (tendency) and predetermination (inevitability). People who develop addiction problems, for example, may have predispositional characteristics such as a low tolerance for coping with unpleasant feelings or frustrations in their life, being sensation-seeking and avoiding boredom, needing instant satisfaction, and displaying 'a pattern of automatic, nonreflective yielding to impulses' (Beck *et al.*, 1993: 39). The implication of predisposition is not to succumb to pessimism, but to employ greater and more sustained effort to overcome the problem or minimise the adverse impact it may have on your life. As Ellis *et al.* point out: 'All behavior is multiply determined and, therefore, clients with strong biological predispositions to a specific problem had better work harder to maximize the influence of psychosocial factors' (1988: 23). Such psychosocial factors might include mixing with people who support your efforts at change and avoiding people or situations that might help to trigger a relapse.

With regard to temperament, you may classify yourself as an introvert or extrovert and say 'This is who I am. That's me' as if your personality cannot shift. However, research suggests that 'we can stretch our personalities, but only up to a point . . . We might call this the "rubber band theory" of personality. We are like rubber bands at rest. We are elastic and can stretch ourselves, but only so much' (Cain: 2012: 117–8). For example, an introvert may shrink from having to stand in the spotlight in order to market his services (as we find with some of our colleagues who want to add coaching to their therapy practice) while an extrovert may baulk at the prospect of solitude in order to complete an important project (as we find with some students' inability to get their dissertations in on time). In both cases, the person decides to 'stretch the band' to achieve important goals.

'What if i'm not successful?'

This usually means that all your efforts at change will have been wasted if you don't achieve your goal. We would suggest that this attitude stems from your philosophy of low frustration tolerance (for example, 'I can't stand the uncertainty of not knowing. I struggle every day to put in all this blasted hard work, then I don't get the promotion. Why should I put myself through that?'). You want a guarantee that your perseverance will pay off and as you know you cannot be given one, this provides the rationale for not pushing yourself. Staying as you are, however, will maintain the same staleness and predictability in your life that you want to change. You can see uncertainty as a challenge instead of being daunted by it. Uncertainty doesn't have to mean negative outcomes – you may put a consistently negative bias into your thinking about uncertainty – and instead of dwelling on these negative outcomes,

> focus your attention on the actual facts that you do know [the eligi-bility criteria for promotion]. If you think that the problem to solve is to solve problems about the unknowable [knowing the outcome before it's occurred such as whether you've got the promotion], then you will feel helpless.
>
> (Leahy, 2006: 106)

'I'm not making progress, so I might as well give up.'

This statement may reflect your disenchantment with change because you're not seeing *immediate* progress as well as reflecting your ambiva-lence about change. You may have declared in your mind that if nothing changes by the end of the week, then there's no point in going on. This reinforces your uncertainty about wanting to change (you might be get-ting pressure from others to do so). When attempting to alter ingrained behaviours, it may be some time before progress is evident or if there is some initial evidence of it, resist the urge to dismiss it as 'insignifi-cant'. Change usually occurs in small steps rather than one giant stride. For example, I (WD) am currently on a healthy eating, weight-loss pro-gramme but am losing weight more slowly than I expected given the nature of the programme. Even though I've had thoughts of giving up, I don't do so because I accept the fact (without liking it) that my body will lose weight at its rate rather than at the rate desired by my mind.

Having contradictory feelings about change (for example, 'I want to, but . . .') doesn't have to prevent you from persevering with it. Being totally and irrevocably committed to change is not usually the stance of most people we coach; it's only a minority who square up to change with ringing declarations of 'going for broke', 'failure is not an option' or 'I've burnt my bridges, there's no going back'. Doubt and uncertainty are the usual concomitants of change. If you wait patiently for progress to emerge and work through your ambivalence about change, then you'll be less likely to give up.

Some coaches and coaching books urge you to eliminate doubt from your goal-directed thinking. We have no idea how to do this or wish to do it. As the philosopher Julian Baggini remarks: 'Our belief that self-belief has to be absolute means that we inevitably see any self-doubt as a sign of weakness to be expunged. In other words, self-doubt undermines will only because we have not learned to live with doubt' (Baggini and Macaro, 2012: 42–3). We believe that self-doubt is part of self-belief as you're not afraid to examine what you're doing or the decisions you've made, and you sometimes conclude that you're wrong and fresh thinking and action are called for.

Commitment to sunk costs

Sunk costs (Leahy, 1999) are the investments (for example, financial, emotional, or vocational) you have made in a particular course of action, such as staying in a relationship that you consider to be 'dead'. You're reluctant to leave the relationship as this means having to justify these failed investments (for example, 'Why didn't I leave much earlier if I wasn't happy?'). To avoid such painful self-scrutiny, you persist with your failed investments (that is, you remain in the relationship). Another example: you're in a job you describe as 'really boring' but leaving it would mean realising how much time and effort you've wasted (for example, 'Ten years down the bloody drain!'), engaging in self-condemnation (for example, 'I'm a failure for wasting ten years of my life in this boring job'), and confronting the risk of an uncertain future as you start again (for example, 'What if the next job turns out the same or I can't even get one?'). Your focus is on looking back to preserve or justify these costs rather than looking forward to new opportunities; in other words, you dig yourself further into the hole (for example, staying in the boring job) instead of trying to climb out of it (for example, looking for a more interesting one).

Rather than any further commitment to sunk costs, you can: (a) ask yourself what constructive lessons you can learn from those 'wasted' years to guide future behaviour; (b) re-evaluate your conclusion that those years were completely wasted (for example, 'The job did pay the mortgage and other bills after all'); (c) consider that some measured risk-taking opens the way for a more exciting or interesting life than always playing it safe; and (d) understand the reasons for your behaviour during those years (for example, 'I was afraid of losing my safety net') instead of seeing it as stemming from personal failure and deficiency.

Jumping from task to task.

We usually see people on a weekly basis for coaching, with them carrying out self-help assignments between sessions. Some individuals expect to be given a new self-help assignment in every session as they assume that 'one lunge' at a problem is sufficient expenditure of effort on it. In fact, you may need to spend several weeks or longer on a particular task before you start thinking, behaving and feeling differently. For example, through a series of exposure tasks you're now able to stay in an anxiety-provoking situation and discover that your fears haven't been realised; up to that point, you always left the situation as soon as you felt anxious. We would suggest that you establish a coping criterion before tackling your next problem. A coping criterion helps you to assess if you've reached the stage of managing your problems rather than mastering them. This assessment can be viewed along three dimensions of relative rather than absolute progress:

1. Frequency – are you experiencing the problem (for example, anger) less frequently than before?
2. Intensity – is the problem experienced less intensely than before?
3. Duration – does the problem last for shorter periods than before?

If the answer is 'yes' to all three questions, then focus on another problem but don't forget to keep an eye on the previous one because if left 'unattended', it might become troublesome again.

Hidden agendas

These are the covert but real reasons why some individuals enter coaching rather than the ostensible ones they state to the coach. Hidden agendas involve you working (or appearing to) on issues that you don't want to resolve. If we detect the presence of a hidden agenda, we suggest to the person what's 'really going on' (that is, we're not focused on the real goal) in an atmosphere of unconditional acceptance of the person as a fallible human being – the person isn't criticised for having a hidden agenda and thereby is more likely to reveal it.

For example, if you were able to tackle constructively your guilt about ending a relationship (for example, 'I will contribute to but not cause his unhappiness if I leave; his emotional reaction is primarily his responsibility, not mine'), accept yourself for pursuing a hidden agenda in coaching (claiming you wanted to save the relationship) and understand the reasons for doing so ('I always thought hurting people meant I was bad'), then you will be better placed to reveal your true intentions and end the relationship, from your viewpoint, on an honest note.

'Change looks after itself, doesn't it?'

You may believe that after a period of sustained effort at tackling a problem successfully (for example, overcoming procrastination), your progress is maintained independently of any further efforts on your part. This is a recipe for relapse: old self-defeating thoughts, feelings and behaviours can 'creep back' and create further problems for you. In order to maintain your gains over the long term, you need to engage in daily practice of your new thoughts and behaviours in order to deepen your conviction in them and simultaneously weaken your adherence to old, unproductive thoughts and behaviours. Once this practice becomes habitual, less effort will be needed for this monitoring function.

'I don't feel any different'

You may complain that after weeks of persistent effort on your part, you still feel down in the dumps even though you grudgingly acknowledge that you're thinking and acting more productively. The seeming intractability of your low mood may convince you to 'throw in the towel'. We would urge you not to do this because emotions take longer to change than thoughts or behaviours (the reasons for this phenomenon are complex). You can liken the change process to a three-horse race. One horse is called 'Behaviour', another is called 'Thinking' and the third is called 'Emotion'. The first two horses always pull ahead while 'Emotion' is a notoriously slow starter but does eventually catch up. So have patience, persist with the change process and you will start to feel differently as your mood improves.

Secondary gains

This refers to individuals who 'have a "vested interest" in maintaining the status quo of the problem because of the "payoffs" that the problem produces' (Cormier and Cormier, 1985: 189). For example, you remain depressed because of the sympathy and attention you receive from others which you believe will stop when you get better; you fail to stop smoking because you fear gaining weight if you do, turning into 'a tub of lard' and becoming an object of ridicule. In both examples, the perceived consequences of change are worse than the problem itself. If you're unsure why your efforts at change are unsuccessful, ask yourself some of the following questions to assess for the presence of secondary gains (Cormier and Cormier, 1985):

1   'The good thing about my problem is . . .'
2   'Has my problem ever produced any special advantages or considerations for me?'
3   'As a consequence of my problem, have I got out of or avoided things or events?'
4   'What do I get out of this situation that I don't get out of other situations?'
5   'How does this problem help me?'

If you want to give up your secondary gains and see your efforts at change bear fruit, then you will need to address the ostensible problem (unable to stop smoking in the above example) and the real or core problem (fear of ridicule from others for being overweight).

'I can see what the problem is now'

You may believe that 'seeing' what the cause of the problem is will automatically resolve it without any further effort from you. Insight alone will bring about the necessary changes in your life. Unfortunately, the change process is more complicated: insight plus forceful and persistent action equals enduring change. For example, you see that your self-worth is dependent upon the approval of others and the solution to this dependency is to value yourself irrespective of how others see you (you believe this new viewpoint lightly and inconsistently). Unless you put this insight into daily practice (for example, being assertive when necessary, doing things that may incur criticism or rejection from others), it's highly unlikely that you'll integrate your new view of self-worth into your belief system (that is, you believe it deeply and consistently).

Insufficient critical thinking

Questioning your ideas using reason – that is, the ability to explain or justify our beliefs and actions as well as changing them for more helpful beliefs and actions, having analysed problems, weighed evidence, conducted experiments, looked at other perspectives, defined terms and drawn conclusions unaffected by bias – is an important skill to learn if you want to become a better problem-solver (we might summarise this as thinking straight instead of crookedly). To be adept at this requires developing and providing well-supported arguments rather than: accepting things at face value; taking refuge in positive thinking; claiming to have been brainwashed into thinking something; relying on blind faith or gut instinct; handing your mind over to others such as a guru to do your thinking for you; or surrendering to mental laziness with a weary 'I don't know' as thinking things through is burdensome (as Bertrand Russell observed: 'Most people would rather die than think, and most people do').

For example, a client says, 'My father told me I would be a failure in life and he was right.' Instead of accepting this 'truth', the client would need to, among other things, ask himself how would he define failure? Would he condemn everyone else in a similar position to himself? Does he think his father was just being wise in predicting his son's destiny or did he have an axe to grind? Are there ways to break free from this self-image of failure?

According to Carol Tavris, tolerating uncertainty 'is probably the hardest step in becoming a critical thinker, for it requires that we hold our beliefs lightly enough [rather than clinging to them] that we can give them up when better evidence comes along' (2011: viii). I (MN) remember Tavris giving a talk in which she spoke about the exhilaration you can feel in giving up a weak argument for a much stronger one. Holding on to a weak argument or problem-perpetuating viewpoint may be because you worry about loss of face if you change your mind (politicians often fear, and their opponents will attack them for it, that policy U-turns will be seen as weakness, as not having faith in their political convictions); you're not sure how to develop or what an alternative viewpoint would look like; or you believe the costs of changing beliefs would be too high in disrupting your self-image or settled world view.

All this talk about reason and critical thinking can give the impression that we want you to be passionless fact-finders endlessly weighing evidence for every step you take. Passion and reason are not enemies but allies: reason keeping a watch on passion as it knows the dangers of passion unrestrained, and passion reminding reason not to forget zest and variety in life. While you may pride yourself on always 'using my head (that is, reason) to guide my actions' it could happen one day that you 'forget your head' (reason takes flight). Crews (2006: 11) warns that 'rationality isn't an endowment but an achievement that can come undone at any moment'. It comes undone when you banish critical thinking – which we've done in the past – and install credulity which is likely to promote adventures that, unfortunately, often end in angry bewilderment, for example, 'How could I have been so stupid in joining that cult which promised unlimited happiness but delivered only misery? Why did I do it?' Persistence in and improving your critical thinking will help to minimise such misadventures.

Coaching example

Paula worked as a therapist and wanted to write an article for a counselling journal (it would be her first attempt). She liked the idea of having the article published but was less enthusiastic about actually writing it because she kept getting 'stuck'. She became fed up with the research she had to do to give the article an academic underpinning, and the amount of time consumed by the article which she'd seriously underestimated ('It's getting in the way of other things I like to do'). She was angry with her slow progress – 'I thought I could knock it out in a couple of weeks' – and seriously considered abandoning the project 'to get some peace of mind'. I (MN) asked her if she really would gain this:

PAULA: No. If I give up I'll give myself a hard time for being such a wimp. I do want to continue but . . .

MICHAEL: But what . . .?

PAULA: It's such a hard slog.

MICHAEL: It may be a hard slog but what attitude do you bring to the task that makes it even harder?

PAULA: Me? Nothing. It's just a hard slog. I'm not sure I understand what you mean.

MICHAEL: When you sit down to write the article, what attitude is in your mind that makes you want to give up instead of pushing on?

PAULA: Oh, I see. Well, 'I hate this hard slog. Things should be easier.'

MICHAEL: Realistically, given this is your first attempt at writing an article and all that goes with it, should it be relatively easy or hard, or even a great struggle?

PAULA: Put like that, it should be hard, not easy. I've obviously got a lot to learn about writing articles. I'd probably say the same as you've done if someone was complaining to me about the difficulties of writing a first article.

MICHAEL: What are the consequences for you of having this 'it's too hard' attitude?

PAULA: I procrastinate a lot or I'm looking for excuses to stop writing and do something more enjoyable. I concentrate more on how bad

I'm feeling than on getting the article done. Of course, the finish date for the article just recedes over the horizon.

MICHAEL: So that attitude doesn't help you to persist with the article to get it finished within a reasonable time.

PAULA: Definitely not.

MICHAEL: So what attitude would be more helpful?

PAULA: Well, keep on reminding myself that it should be hard writing my first article or a second or third if I ever get around to it.

MICHAEL: It's not just sitting in a chair reminding yourself that it should be hard because then you might go and do something else as a reward for accepting this fact.

PAULA: Okay, that's true. Keep on reminding myself while I'm actually working on the article. Rewards come after I've done some work.

MICHAEL: Right.

To encapsulate this new outlook, Paula nicknamed herself 'Persevering Paula'. She allotted some time most days to work on the article. She finished it three months' later and sent it off to the journal. When she received a reply from the journal she became down-hearted: 'They've accepted it subject to some changes and improvements. Those blasted anonymous reviewers. More work!' I asked her if 'Persevering Paula' was just going to be around for three months or lifelong. 'Alright, I get the point,' she said. She revised the article, sent it off and was informed that it would be published within a year to eighteen months.

PAULA: I'm pissed off again. I hoped it would be published in a couple of months so I could see the fruit of my labours.

MICHAEL: Some journals will fast-track certain articles but obviously not yours. So you will need to learn patience, of which one dictionary definition is 'tolerant perseverance or forbearance'.

PAULA: (laughs) Oh no, perseverance again! I suppose I could write another article while I'm waiting.

MICHAEL: Now there's a thought.

Conclusion

We've emphasised in this chapter the central importance of being persistent in pursuit of your goals, and discussed what can block you from developing this outlook. Not persisting involves a paradox: your persistence at not persisting (won't power instead of willpower) is likely to create more problems for you in the longer term which will then require your persistence in tackling them. The next time you baulk at persisting with an activity that's important to you, remember that the consequences of not persevering with it are likely to be worse than tolerating the uncomfortable struggle of 'sticking with it'. Finally, our persistence can help us to see that 'it is not what we get but what we become by our endeavours that makes them worthwhile' (Grayling, 2002: 39). As one client said (echoing others): 'Of course there was satisfaction in reaching my goal but the greater pleasure, a revelation really, was the unexpected grit I had to see it through.'

Chapter 6

Dealing with criticism

Introduction

'You're hopeless!' How would you cope if someone said that to you? Get angry, verbally or physically lash out, agree with the person, become depressed and withdrawn, feel hurt and sulk or, with poise and coolness, ask for clarification ('When you say "you're hopeless", what do you mean by that specifically')? Why is it that criticism can bounce off you one day then apparently crush you the next? When we see people for coaching, one of the things that most of them ask us is how to handle and respond to criticism constructively (for example, 'When my boss starts ticking me off, instead of listening I keep thinking "drop dead". Why can't I focus on what he's saying to me? There's usually some truth in it').

Being on the receiving end of criticism (even if it's well intentioned) can touch a raw nerve or leave you feeling vulnerable. As we have argued in other chapters of this book, it's not the situation itself (in this case, being criticised) that determines how you feel, but how you think about the situation or criticism. For example:

A – activating event: your friend says to you that you can be spiteful at times.

B – beliefs and thoughts: 'She shouldn't say that about me. She's supposed to be my friend! It's like she's stabbed me in the back. I've been a good friend to her. What did I do to deserve this?'

C – emotional and behavioural consequences: you're hurt and you withdraw from your friend's company thereby shutting down channels of communication (sulking).

You may protest that you didn't want to feel hurt and wouldn't seek something you didn't want; therefore, her criticism of you caused you to feel hurt. This argument is often called the common sense view of emotional causation (more colloquially, 'the bleedin' obvious') or A-C thinking (events or others determine our emotional reactions). We would argue differently. You can think of yourself at B as a gatekeeper: you choose what to keep out or let in. Instead of rejecting her criticism you allow it in; then you have another choice regarding how you're going to process her comments (for example, reflect on what she said to see if there's any truth in it and what your measured response will be, or bridle with indignation that your character has been attacked).

In the above example, you've let your friend's comments in and chosen to evaluate them in the following way: denying her freedom of expression ('She shouldn't say that about me'); insisting she should act in a way deemed appropriate by you ('She's supposed to be my friend!'); viewing her comments as an act of treachery – the ultimate betrayal ('It's like she's stabbed me in the back'); seeing friendship only in terms of what you've done ('I've been a good friend to her'); and considering yourself to be 'special' in some way so this shouldn't happen to you ('What did I do to deserve this?'). Your thoughts at B reflect the theme in hurt: you've been let down or betrayed by another and you're undeserving of such treatment; in other words, you've been treated unfairly by her comments. Therefore, B, not A, led to C (B–C thinking: your reactions to events are largely determined by your thoughts and beliefs). Imagine looking at the same situation in a different way:

A – activating event: your friend says to you that you can be spiteful at times.
B – beliefs and thoughts: 'I wonder why she said that? Maybe I've said or done something she's not happy about. The best way to find out is to ask her and clear the air. I am surprised by her comment though.'
C – emotional and behavioural consequences: you're annoyed but you remain in contact with her thereby keeping channels of communication open.

A is the same but is viewed differently by you at B which produces new changes at C. Whether criticism of you is fair or unfair, you're still responsible for your reaction to it. Once this insight into emotional causation has been grasped, you can then decide if you want to continue to respond to criticism in a 'touchy' way or be robust in dealing with it. We now discuss some of the ways people upset themselves when they're criticised.

The approval junkie (Forward, 1997)

While receiving approval from others, particularly significant others, is a pleasant experience, believing you *need* their approval, you cannot survive or be happy without it, places you in a subordinate position (Forward, 1997). For example, Jennifer was afraid when her boyfriend was upset because he wouldn't speak to her and this meant she no longer had his approval. As Forward says: 'The approval junkie's motto is, "If I'm not getting approval, I've done something wrong". Or worse yet, "If I'm not getting approval there's something wrong with me"' (1997: 167). Jennifer always believed it was her fault that he was upset, begged to be told what she'd done wrong and how she could put it right in order to be approved of again (that is, receive her approval 'fix'). I (MN) asked Jennifer what happened when her partner criticised her:

JENNIFER: When he says things like 'You're getting on my nerves' or 'You're no good in bed', I sort of collapse inside, devastated.

MICHAEL: What thoughts are going through your mind when you 'collapse inside'?

JENNIFER: It's always the same: he doesn't want me any more, he's fed up with me.

MICHAEL: And if that's true, what does that mean to you?

JENNIFER: If he doesn't want me then I can't be any good.

MICHAEL: When you say 'I can't be any good', what does that mean about you?

JENNIFER: *(voice drops)* That I'm worthless.

MICHAEL: So is the formula something like this: criticism proves you're worthless while approval means you're acceptable . . . temporarily?

JENNIFER: That's right. I'll do anything for him to be acceptable again. Really pathetic, isn't it?

Criticism per se doesn't make you upset: the meaning you attach to it does; in Jennifer's case, criticism means she's worthless. As Eleanor Roosevelt observed: 'No one can make you feel inferior without your consent.' If you are an approval junkie, you continually give your consent to be made to feel inferior because you already believe it about yourself.

In order to wean yourself off your approval 'fix' and stand up to criticism instead of allowing it to crush you, it's important to internalise self-acceptance, that is, never rating yourself, only your actions or traits, for example, 'My behaviour may get on your nerves sometimes but I refuse to put myself down because of it'; 'You say I'm no good in bed. Well, there isn't much sexual chemistry between us but that doesn't make me no good – in or out of bed.' Decoupling your actions from yourself allows you to be problem-focused (for example, 'What aspects of myself require some changes and do I want to stay in this relationship?') instead of self-focused (for example, 'What's wrong with me?'). We would argue that coping with and responding to criticism constructively rests on a bedrock of self-acceptance. Jennifer forcefully and persistently worked at accepting herself, warts and all (for example, 'I can accept myself for desperately needing his approval, but it's something about myself which I don't like and which I'm determined to change'). A word of caution is needed here about self-acceptance. You can only really strive towards ever greater self-acceptance. We're not suggesting that you can achieve full self-acceptance once and for all. That's like saying you have achieved fully clean teeth and don't ever have to brush them again!

She came to see clearly the differences between needs and desires. Needs are based on demands: what you believe you *must* have in order to be happy or see yourself as having some worth. This rigid outlook doesn't really make you happy or convince you of your worth because you're usually anxious about losing your partner's approval, depressed if you do and often self-hating for being so weak. Desires are based on preferences: what you would like to have but don't insist that you must have in order to be happy or worthwhile. Jennifer had developed new perspectives on herself, the relationship and her partner:

JENNIFER: When he criticises me now, I no longer collapse like before. I ask specifically what it is about my behaviour he's unhappy with and then I consider if his criticisms are warranted. I also do the previously unthinkable and criticise his behaviour which unnerves him. In fact, he seems at times to need my approval but I don't want to play games with him like he did with me. Now I see things clearly, I will probably leave the relationship as it has nothing to offer me any longer. I've taken off my shackles which I put on, not him.

MICHAEL: Is it just the relationship you're seeing in a different light?

JENNIFER: No, there are other areas of my life like with my parents or work colleagues where I still need my approval fix . . . but not for much longer.

MICHAEL: Because . . .?

JENNIFER: Because being criticised doesn't have to hurt unless you let it – it may sting at times but no more than that.

Jennifer's need for approval was based on a fear of disapproval and what that would mean about her. However, if you only fear active disapproval you would not be too concerned at mere lack of approval. Why? As Dryden and Gordon explain: 'Because not getting approval is not the same as getting active disapproval. In other words, a neutral response would be OK; it wouldn't bother you' (1993: 66). If a neutral response did bother you, then it's likely you're interpreting it as some form of implied criticism (for example, 'She's not bothered about me either way. What am I to her – a nonentity or something?') and therefore you conclude you're being disapproved of. You might be the kind of person who *has* to know if you're being actively approved or disapproved of before you can evaluate yourself (for example, 'She likes me, I'm OK; she doesn't like me, I'm not OK').

Rejection

While the fear of rejection hangs in the air for people who need the approval of others, being rejected can often be seen as the most devastating form of criticism – you're no longer wanted or desired. When John's girlfriend left him after five years together, he described the experience as like 'being kicked in the stomach, then thrown in the dustbin labelled "reject"'. He attributed his depressed reaction entirely to being dumped by his girlfriend whereas, in fact, there are two phases to rejection. Firstly, someone else rejects you; secondly, you reject yourself (in John's case, 'Without her, I'm nothing'). As Hauck points out: 'We can be rejected by others and still not reject ourselves. It is when *we* reject *ourselves* that we get into emotional trouble, not when others reject us' (1981a: 8; emphasis in original). The harshest criticism came from John, not his departing girlfriend. She did list a lot of his faults but, as he admitted, she never called him worthless (even if she had done, he doesn't have to agree with her evaluation of him).

John saw and accepted that he was really suffering from self-rejection (which is not to minimise the unhappiness involved in the end of a five-year relationship). The realisation that his worth and happiness rested largely in his hands rather than someone else's, gave him the confidence to ask women out, handle rejection from them without rejecting himself in the process and eventually find a new partner.

Defensiveness

Defensiveness is a common reaction to being criticised. Instead of letting in and mulling over another's criticisms of you to determine if there's any truth in them, you may resort to rationalising your behaviour (that is, engaging in plausible but specious reasoning). For example, say a friend of yours mentions in passing that you talk about yourself a great deal. Initially shocked, you quickly respond by saying that you only do it to start a conversation or fill in the silences, poke fun at yourself to get people in a lighter mood and add sarcastically: 'Of course, you never ever talk about yourself, do you?' If you were to face the criticism head-on you may find some unpalatable truth in it, (for example, 'I suppose she's right to a certain extent. I do like to be the centre of attention, but I feel that people will be interested in me and my experiences in life'). Even though you try to explain away your friend's criticisms (for example, 'She's going through a divorce, so she's taking it out on me'), you gradually phase her out of your life because 'we don't have much in common anyway' instead of admitting the real reason: 'How dare she criticise me like that! I thought she was my friend; instead she turns out to be a snake in the grass.'

If you put aside your defensiveness, then you can engage in rational thinking, not rationalisation. For instance, you now believe your friends can criticise you and even though you may not like what they say, you will listen to the criticisms and evaluate them dispassionately (for example, 'It's true that I do talk about myself a lot and I'm aware that some of my friends and associates do, at times, avoid my company because of it') and decide on a course of action to initiate change in your life (for example, 'I do want better friendships, so I will work hard to make conversations with them more evenly balanced instead of largely one-sided'). Finally, you no longer equate your behaviour with yourself (for example, 'I may act selfishly at times but that doesn't make me a selfish person, just a person who refuses to rate herself on the basis of her behaviour'). Such rational thinking can help you to be open to criticism without necessarily agreeing with it and avoiding acting defensively.

Getting angry

We often hear people tell us that anger is a natural reaction when responding to criticism, 'How else am I supposed to feel? Throw my arms around him?' Often the ideas behind such anger run something like this: 'He shouldn't criticise me. That bastard should keep his mouth shut!' Brian felt angry with his boss when he criticised a presentation he'd made: 'Who does that bastard think he is criticising me like that? His presentations are not so hot. Maybe I should give him a piece of my mind.' I (MN) asked Brian if he believed in freedom of speech:

BRIAN: Of course I do. That's one of the important things about a democracy. What's that got to do with this issue?

MICHAEL: The relevance is this: if you believe in freedom of speech, why did you get so angry when your boss criticised your presentation?

BRIAN: Well, he was being downright unfair, completely out of order. I thought the presentation was alright.

MICHAEL: Let's assume for the moment that his comments were unfair, why isn't your boss allowed to say things that are unfair?

BRIAN: He damn well shouldn't that's why! He should keep his bloody opinions to himself.

MICHAEL: Aren't you denying him freedom of speech with those 'shoulds' and damning him in the process? You don't have to like or agree with his comments, but is he allowed to make them?

BRIAN: *(long pause)* I want to say no, but if I really do believe in freedom of speech, which I do, then the answer has to be yes.

Brian's restrictions on free speech in this instance are determined by his emotional upset about his boss's comments. By pointing out the conflict between his support of free speech and his dictatorial 'shoulds', Brian was able to develop a new perspective on his boss's criticisms: 'His comments may be unfair but he has the right to make them. He is my boss after all. I can listen to them without upsetting myself about them. I was wrong to call him a bastard for saying things I didn't like.'

Sometimes people can say or do things that appear to attack your self-esteem and you verbally lash out at them in retaliation. This is called ego-defensive anger. For example, you pride yourself on always meeting deadlines but on this occasion you're going to miss it. A colleague pops in to see you and tut-tuts: 'Oh dear, your report is going to be late. Whatever next?' You reply angrily: 'Get stuffed, go away and let me get on.' Whether your colleague meant to or not, he has publicly revealed what you consider to be a weakness – failure to meet the deadline. By attacking your colleague you're able to put off, but not for long, unsettling self-examination (for example, 'I'm not so efficient after all as a team leader and he's rubbed my nose in that fact').

The first question to ask is: would you have been angry with your colleague if you didn't consider missing a deadline to be a weakness? Using a specific incident to label your role, an inefficient team leader, is a 'part equals the whole' error in thinking – you can *only* ever be an inefficient team leader (it's important to remember that devaluation in some cases can be linked just to the role without encompassing the self as well). If some of your colleagues do indeed regard you as inefficient for falling below your standards, you can remind yourself that they're also making the 'part–whole' error which is probably no more helpful to them when they reveal their weaknesses as it was to you when you revealed yours (incidentally, management-speak these days likes to talk of development possibilities or opportunities rather than weaknesses).

The philosopher A. C. Grayling states that conflict and resentment are inevitable in life, so we need a rule to govern what things we can say and those things we should not say:

> So the rule is this: never asperse [attack or criticise] people for what they physically cannot help being. By all means attack what they choose to think or be; but even here it is better to attack ideas rather than individuals. Best of all, don't attack anyone for anything until you have given them a proper hearing. But if, having done so, you think they speak falsehood, folly or malice, do not be afraid to say so with all the eloquence and determination you can muster.
>
> (2010: 176–7)

Hurt

We discussed hurt at the beginning of this chapter but would now like to expand on the concept of deservingness found in hurt. This occurs when someone has made comments or performed actions that you perceive to be uncaring (for example, 'I don't deserve to be told that I'm holding him back after years of my support and loyalty to him'). No matter how much you love or respect someone or what you've done for him or her, there's no law of the universe which states that they cannot make unkind or uncaring comments about you or that you have some special status in the world that exempts you from receiving such criticisms. Sulking is the usual behavioural response when you feel hurt and one of its functions is to try and make your partner feel guilty for his hurtful comments and thereby induce him to make amends for them.

Even though the world would probably be a better place to live in if considerate and caring behaviour was always reciprocated, unfortunately this isn't the case. Accepting that your belief of deservingness is shared by no one else is the first step in developing a non-upsetting and asser-tive response to criticism (for example, 'I don't like the way you speak to me sometimes but sulking is not the way to deal with it. I want to find out what's going on with you. Now, what do you mean by "I'm holding you back"'?).

Constant criticism

You may know certain people in your life (for example, colleague, boss) who constantly criticise you and, understandably, you may get worn down by it and even convince yourself that you must have some serious character defect to invite so much sustained criticism. Not so. These people are chronic complainers, whiners who

> gripe *ad nauseam* about anything and everything. Believing themselves to be powerless to take control of their own lives, these people firmly believe the world *should be* this way, or *should not be* that way, and that you and/or other people should do something about it!
>
> (Dryden and Gordon, 1994: 33; italics in original)

Raymond worked with a colleague who was a chronic complainer. He tried several strategies to deal with the problem which proved unsuccessful: ignoring the complaints, avoiding the complainer or trading complaint for complaint. In our coaching sessions, I (MN) suggested to Raymond a different approach of taking the wind out of the complainer's sails:

MICHAEL: *(as complainer)* Your work is always poor.
RAYMOND: You think my work is always poor. In what specific ways is my work always poor?
 [Raymond acknowledges the criticism and then asks for clarification of it.]
MICHAEL: *(impatiently)* What do you mean 'specific ways'? Your work is always poor. What else is there to say?
RAYMOND: I don't agree that my work is always poor but sometimes I do perform poorly which is true, so it would be helpful to me if you could pinpoint specific areas for discussion.
 [Raymond decides what's true and false regarding the criticism and persists with his request for specific information.]
MICHAEL: Trying to be clever are you? Well for starters, your phone calls.
RAYMOND: What is the precise problem with the phone calls?
MICHAEL: They go on for too long. You're never off that bloody phone.
RAYMOND: I agree that I do spend too much time on the phone with some of the customers, so what specific suggestions can you offer me to improve my telephone skills?

[Raymond puts the complainer on the spot by asking for advice.]
MICHAEL: *(irritably)* You either know what to do or you don't!
RAYMOND: I'm afraid that isn't a helpful reply. Maybe I could sit in with
  you on some of your phone calls and learn that way.
  [As the complainer is proving unhelpful, Raymond models for him
  how to offer a specific suggestion.]
MICHAEL: There is always a smart-arse in every office. What's the point
  in trying to help you? It's not going to make any difference anyway. There's nothing else to say. You've exhausted me with your
  attitude.
RAYMOND: I'm sorry you feel like that, but I would appreciate any further complaints you make about me to be specific in nature and,
  if justified, are then followed by your constructive suggestions for
  improvement. Otherwise your complaints are a waste of time for
  both of us.

Following this new strategy, Raymond noticed a sharp reduction in the
number of complaints he received from the 'complainer': 'Always asking him to be specific about his complaints was the way to deal with him.
He's on somebody else's case now.' As Mann points out: 'Constant criticism invariably says more about the (jealous or insecure) source of the
comments than it does about you' (1998: 59). We would suggest that with
any criticism made against you, instead of making yourself angry over it,
analyse the criticism by asking yourself two questions: 'Is it true?' and
'Is it false?' If it's true (for example, 'I do drink too much'), then admit
it without self-condemnation and decide if you wish to pursue a course
of remedial action (for example, reducing your intake of alcohol). If it's
false (for example, 'I definitely keep to the recommended weekly units'),
then let the person have the right to be wrong about you without damning
him for his errors of judgement, and then get on with something more
enjoyable. Remember that you too have the right to be wrong about others without damning yourself for having poor judgement at times.

Oversensitivity to criticism

In the above example, if you tried to convince the other person that he
was wrong about your drinking patterns, why would you need to do that?
Why can't you let the matter rest? You have made his error a problem for
yourself. You may easily take offence whether criticism is intended or
not (for example, 'I don't dye my hair. What's he going on about?') and
try to always put the record straight about yourself (for example, 'Look,

I'm not a worrier just because I ask you if we're going to get there on time'). In both cases, other people have to see you in the same way you like to portray yourself, but the general impression among your friends and colleagues is that you're 'touchy' which is not how you want to be seen.

Such oversensitivity to criticism often stems from a tension between our inner and outer selves and others' comments can prompt troubling self-scrutiny (for example, 'I do worry a lot but why should I admit it to her? I can't help it. I don't want to be this way. Why has she got to point out I'm a worrier and make me look neurotic?'). To curb this problem, do your best not to use others' comments as a stick to beat yourself with, accept that there are aspects of yourself that you don't like and want to change and allow others to have their own opinion of you which, of course, you can challenge or question if you believe the context requires it. By becoming much less sensitive to criticism you may find that some of it is actually helpful when you listen to it in a non-troubled state (for example, a friend tells you he used to be a 'worryguts' and how he over-came it like you can too, which inspires hope in you). After all, one of the key ways of developing self-awareness is to ask for, accept and act on constructive criticism particularly when everyone is pointing out the same problem with your behaviour.

Shame

You may fear actual or potential criticism because your faults will be exposed to the scrutiny of others; this scrutiny will result in their likely disapproval of you. Shame results from social disapproval (this is why shame is often called a social emotion and we discussed it in Chapter 1). The crucial ingredient in the activation of shame is whether you agree with the actual or imagined disapproval of you by others. For example, you regard yourself as cool under pressure but you lose your temper at a meeting and storm out. Office gossip paints you as 'hysterical' and 'a loose canon'. You feel ashamed because *you agree* with these descriptions of yourself – you have undermined your public image of being cool under pressure by behaving 'hysterically'. Would you worry about los-ing your cool if no one else was there to observe it? If you say 'yes', you might also experience internal shame as you're falling well below your internalised ideal standard of behaviour.

To tackle shame, it's important not to judge yourself on the basis of your behaviour (for example, 'I did behave badly at the meeting which I regret, but that doesn't make me "hysterical", "a loose canon" or any other degrading label') and to make self-acceptance independent of the approval of others. You can put these ideas into practice by being open about some of your faults in relevant contexts; in other words, challenging your shame-proneness thinking (for example, 'I want to apologise to everyone at this meeting for my behaviour last week. I'm not sure why I went off the deep end like that – maybe I was under some strain at the time – but I will do my best to ensure that it doesn't happen again'). By internalising self-acceptance, you don't have to maintain your public image at all times in order to save face or worry about falling below your ideal behaviour because it will no longer mean a loss of face, just the inevitable disappointments of being a fallible human being.

Dealing with the inner critic

Your harshest critic is often yourself. Others may put the boot in, but when you give yourself a 'good kicking' your boots are steel toe-capped. You observe yourself pitilessly and pass scathing judgements such as 'Can't you get anything right you stupid idiot?' or 'You'll never have any friends'. You may believe that such attacks on yourself will motivate you to get out of your current difficulties, but these attacks are usually counterproductive as they reinforce your negative self-image when no progress is made or setbacks occur. Your inner critic cannot be appeased because it's contaminated by self-prejudice (Padesky, 1993), that is, your negative self-image (for example, 'I'm incompetent at everything') is maintained firmly in the face of contradictory evidence that could discredit it (for example, 'It doesn't matter how good I am at my job: I didn't get the promotion and that's what counts and that's why I'm incompetent'). Once you realise how bigoted your inner critic is, start to answer back in a constructive and compassionate way:

INNER CRITIC: You're a failure. Just accept it.

INNER COUNSEL: If I accept it, then that means I'll keep on listening to you. You're no help to me.

INNER CRITIC: Stop running away from the truth about yourself.

INNER COUNSEL: Your so-called truth is destructive and will drag me down even further. I know what you suffer from, I read about it – 'it–me' confusion (Gilbert, 1997).

INNER CRITIC: What are you going on about? You're the one that's confused.

INNER COUNSEL: I can only accept *me* if I do *it* well. Because I didn't get the promotion therefore I'm a failure. That's a trap I now wish to avoid. From now on, I'm not going to label 'me' on the basis of 'it'.

INNER CRITIC: Another false dawn for you.

INNER COUNSEL: I prefer to see it as the beginning of my enlightenment and your eventual termination. I've listened to you for long enough.

To answer your inner critic, write down your self-attacking statements and challenge each one in a self-helping way. If you find this difficult to do initially, imagine your friend's inner critic and how you would help her respond to the 'charges' (for example, 'Susan, how does the failure of your daughter's marriage make you a bad mother? Where did you get the power from to control your daughter's destiny? If you could control it, then the marriage wouldn't have ended'). The start of this inner healing 'is to sort out our relationships with ourselves' (Gilbert, 1997:119). Your inner critic survives on the oxygen of self-depreciation, so cut off its supply by learning compassionate self-acceptance.

So far in this book we've focused on challenging or examining the content of your upsetting thinking but there are other ways of dealing with the inner critic. Recent developments in CBT have introduced mindfulness techniques. Mindfulness is observing your thoughts in the present moment without judging them. Mindfulness teaches you how to change your relationship to these thoughts, not to challenge them. Upsetting thoughts can appear stronger than they actually are because we keep arguing or pleading with them, obsessing about or trying to suppress them, relaxing them away or exhorting ourselves to think positive – all to no avail as we've become prisoners of our thinking. Now just imagine you had a belief, 'I'm no good', and you observed it without engaging with it, the belief has become detached from yourself. If you leave the belief alone (a do nothing strategy) it will eventually wither away through neglect. Every time you engage with the belief you give it credibility because you wouldn't be engaging with it if it didn't seem credible to you!

You're not expected to sit there all day observing your thoughts (just as you're not expected to challenge your upsetting thoughts all the time), so get on with your valued activities while accepting the thoughts are still with you; it's important to remember that these activities are not to be used as a form of avoidance of or distraction from the thoughts. For example, Leahy (2010: 75) says that when you go out for a walk and the thoughts intrude:

> You can welcome the thought. You can ask the thought to come along for a walk . . . As you walk along, with the negative thought chattering away and criticizing you, you can decide to accept that it is there. You can even ask it to join you in observing. You can say, "Let's look around at what is in front of us on this walk." . . . Your negative thought may still be with you, but you are walking along in the present moment, observing and accepting the reality in front of you.

Obviously Leahy has engaged with the thought by talking to it but in a neutral way; however, he's not bothered by whatever the thought says or does. You might be wondering when to challenge thoughts or just to be mindfully aware of them. It depends on your preference: you may want to examine your troubling thoughts as you believe there is still some truth or usefulness to them and you like the discussion that ensues or you know there's no point hanging on to them and opt for a mindfulness approach.

Before we leave the topic of mindfulness, let me (WD) share with you how I explain it to people. Imagine you're walking down the road and someone working for a charity greets you with a big smile to which you respond and asks you for a moment of your time. Not wanting to be rude, you stop – only to be locked into a discussion about the good work the charity does and the importance of signing a direct debit to support it. Now imagine a different version of events. The same charity worker smiles at you and asks you to stop. This time you give no response and continue walking. The worker walks by your side talking to you, you know he's there but you continue to give no response. What will he do? Our guess is that he will give up after a while when he sees that he's not getting your attention.

So, in the first version, you engaged with the charity worker and got stuck, but in the second version you didn't engage or get stuck despite the worker trying to get your attention. That's mindfulness: knowing that your inner critic is chuntering on but you choose not to engage with it. After a while, your inner critic will fade away because you haven't responded to it.

To find out more about mindfulness, see Williams and Penman (2011).

Performance evaluation

While your performance is continually evaluated in a variety of contexts (for example, social, sexual, sports), we will limit this discussion to work-based evaluation. This can occur on an informal daily basis through comments passed by your boss, co-workers or customers, or at a formal performance review. Whether you consider appraisal of your performance to be fair or unfair, mild or harsh, how you think about the appraisal is the crucial determinant of your response to it. Some examples: your boss says your performance is generally good but points out some shortcomings which you make yourself upset about (for example, 'I haven't received a flawless appraisal. My performance isn't perfect. I'm a failure'); you receive negative feedback and conclude that you're unlikeable; and your boss makes abusive comments (for example, 'You're no good. You won't make it in this company') which you get angry about (for example, 'How dare he talk to me like that! It's character assassination').

In order to cope with performance evaluation, start with examining your own evaluations (for example, 'If I was performing perfectly, then I wouldn't need a performance review. As this is not the case, I should focus on improving my performance. Calling myself a failure will get in the way of that focus'). Receiving negative feedback and concluding that you are unlikeable on the basis of it are two separate events (external and internal) that you join together; even if your boss doesn't like you, it should not unduly trouble you as long as her feedback is objective (if it's not, you can point out to her the animosity informing her appraisal).

If you have a boss who makes derogatory comments about you, instead of responding in kind, accept that he can act like this (the proof? – because this is undoubtedly how he is acting) and that you will not upset yourself about his probable disturbance. Be persistent in attempting to shape his agenda into something resembling a performance appraisal (for example, 'You keep talking in generalities which is, as I'm sure you know, detrimental to any performance appraisal. Now, again, in what specific ways am I allegedly 'no good'? If you cannot provide any examples today, shall we postpone this meeting until you can?'). By forcing him to put up or shut up, he may get the message that the performance review is his, not yours.

Expressing criticism

The shoe is now on the other foot: you're expressing criticism instead of receiving it. How would you cope if the other person was hurt or angered by your criticism? John's wife, Sue, asked his opinion of the new dress she was wearing to a party: 'It's a bit short, isn't it? It would look better on a younger woman and anyway, you haven't got the legs for it,' he replied. Sue called him a 'bastard' and stormed out of the room. She spent that night in the spare room. John felt very guilty for upsetting Sue and tried to make amends for it by taking her out to dinner and stating that the dress did suit her after all (such insincere apologies did not console her). While John may appear to be the villain in this story, it is actually more complex than that. John's guilt stemmed from two conclusions:

1.   he did something bad – 'I shouldn't have said those things to her';
2.   and he's a bad person for what he said – 'She's right: I am a bastard.'

John is responsible for his feelings and his wife is responsible for hers. While his comments were remarkably tactless to say the least, they also triggered ideas that belonged to his wife (for example, 'He's really telling me I'm old and unattractive. He wants some young bimbo who's got great legs') which then led her to feeling hurt (for example, 'Why is he being so horrible to me?'). If Sue had not felt so insecure, she may have said instead: 'What do you know? I look a knockout, so don't get jealous this evening if I get chatted up at the party.' Your comments can contribute greatly to a person's emotional reaction but he/she, not you, is ultimately responsible for it. Having said that, don't get carried away with the idea that because people largely upset themselves, you can say whatever you like without a care in the world for their reaction. We strongly recommend that you criticise constructively:

• Judge the behaviour or performance, not the person (or, in the above example, the dress rather than the person wearing it), for example, 'I want to comment on some aspects of your workshop presentation. This is not a criticism of you.'
• Be specific and factual in your comments, for example, 'Your workshop evaluations show that one of the main complaints was that there wasn't enough time for questions.'
• Don't dwell on past mistakes or behaviour but focus on how present changes will bring future improvements, for example, 'Time for questions is usually an essential part of a workshop for gaining feedback on how well people are digesting the material and what adjustments may be needed to the content and pacing of the workshop. Does that sound reasonable to you?'
• Listen attentively so that you can discern if the person has any difficulties with or objections to the proposed changes, for example,

'You seem hesitant about implementing these changes. Do you foresee any difficulties that I have overlooked?'

- Acknowledge that you have heard and understood what has been said to you, not merely the words themselves but the *meaning* of them, for example, 'I appreciate some of your worries about these changes but, if I hear you right, you don't want to do any more workshops until you've done some training in workshop presentations. You're fed up with being thrown in at the deep end. Does that seem an accurate summary?'

- Express yourself assertively, that is, without diffidence or anger and attempt to achieve a satisfactory outcome or compromise for both parties, for example, 'In order to improve your workshop performance and increase audience satisfaction, I will arrange some workshop training for you. Then we can assess the impact of the training on your future workshops and discuss any further issues that may have arisen' (see Chapter 7 for a discussion of assertiveness).

As Dryden and Gordon point out:

> Criticizing someone's performance or behaviour is not an end in itself; constructive criticism has a goal. That goal is to change the way a job is being done, or to change some aspect of a person's performance, or to bring about a change in behaviour.
>
> (1994: 57)

The next time you express criticism of someone, ask yourself if you have that goal in mind. Calling a colleague 'a lazy sack of shit' for not pulling his weight in the office would suggest not.

Conclusion

Criticism of you is inevitable; even Mother Teresa did not escape scot-free (see Hitchens, 1995). The important question is how to respond to it without upsetting yourself about it. We would suggest that you: learn self-acceptance by not judging yourself on the basis of your behaviour, only evaluate your behaviour or attitudes; assess the degree of truth in each criticism of you and don't be afraid to admit your mistakes or short-comings; and then consider what changes you need to make to achieve your desired improvements. Constructive criticism can help your self-development, so welcome it.

Chapter 7

Assertiveness

Introduction

It can be galling to be told when recounting a story of someone's impolite behaviour towards you, and how you got upset about it, 'Oh stand up for yourself. Be assertive, not a crybaby.' You may experience a triple dose of resentment: towards the person who was impolite; towards your friend for being unsympathetic; and towards yourself for acting passively and reluctantly acknowledging that your friend's comments had 'the sting of truth'. I (MN) remember a client complaining to me that she was always being told to stand up for herself but no one actually explained how to do it: 'Is it supposed to come to me in a vision? Others said that the worm will finally turn one day and I had to go and look that up as I didn't know what they were talking about.' Being assertive can seem simple, but deceptively so as we shall see. Before we have a look at assertiveness, it's important to point out that, traditionally, assertion training has been applied to areas such as conflict, exploitation, marginalisation, depression, anger, passivity, injustice – the unpleasant side of life. However, being assertive also includes the expression of positive feelings towards others but the person is reluctant to do so, for example, 'I think my boss has done a wonderful job on the project and I would like to say so but I'm worried that my colleagues will see me as a crawler.'

While we emphasise standing up for yourself in this chapter, also remember to stand up to yourself, that is, the self giving instructions to the self, such as getting on with important tasks you've been avoiding or making sure to include pleasurable activities in a heavy work schedule. In this way, the self acts as a mentor and protector to keep your life in balance.

Distinguishing between assertion, aggression and unassertiveness

The first step is understanding the differences between these three concepts and is often called discrimination training. Hauck defines assertion 'as standing up for one's rights *without* anger' and aggression 'as standing up for one's rights *with* anger' (1991a: 207; italics in original). When you act assertively you recognise that the other person has rights also and you hope to achieve a satisfactory result for both sides (a win-win outcome; see Box 7.1). However, this will not always be the case. For example, through persistent assertiveness your neighbour finally and resentfully stops carousing late at night with his friends outside your bedroom window; it's doubtful he will think he has won anything in the exchange.

Aggression involves you acting in an intimidating, demeaning, controlling, manipulating or demanding manner. Only your rights count – your aim is to come out on top at the expense of the other person (a win-lose outcome). Jakubowski and Lange (1978: 69–70) list nine beliefs that promote aggressive behaviour:

- I must win in order to be OK.
- If I don't come on strong, I won't be listened to.
- The world is hostile, and I must be aggressive in order to get ahead in life.

Box 7.1 Some assertive rights

The right to say 'no'
The right to make mistakes
The right to consider my needs important
The right to express my feelings in an appropriate manner without violating anybody else's rights
The right to take responsibility for my actions
The right not to be understood
The right to set my own priorities
The right to respect myself
The right to be me
The right to be assertive without feeling guilty

(Source: Palmer and Dryden, 1995)

- To compromise is to lose.
- I must make an impact.
- I must get my way.
- Aggression is the only way to get through to some people.
- I must prove I'm right and they're wrong.
- The world must be fair; it's intolerable when people mistreat me.

So when you engage in what you assume is assertive behaviour, is your intent to offer your opinion to others or force it on them? And is the outcome likely to be some sort of compromise or the humiliation of the other person?

Unassertiveness 'involves violating one's own rights by failing to express honest feelings, thoughts, and beliefs, or expressing one's thoughts and feelings in such an apologetic, diffident, self-effacing manner that others can easily disregard them' (Lange and Jakubowski, 1976: 9). The message often conveyed by your unassertiveness is: 'I don't really count; what others want is much more important.' Unassertiveness can appear in the guise of politeness, for example, 'Politeness is an expression of good manners and avoids unpleasantness.' However, your internal self-talk might not be so polite as you berate yourself for failing to say what was really on your mind. It's important in assessing unassertiveness to determine if it's a trait (that is, part of your personality) or situation-specific (for example, only with your boss) as this will give an indication of the extent of your interpersonal difficulties.

At first blush, aggression and unassertiveness seem very different behavioural approaches to tackling problematic situations, yet they have something in common: both are based on a threat to a person's self-esteem. For example, you avoid conflict with your partner because this might lead to the withdrawal of his approval, confirming in your mind your worthlessness; a colleague criticises some of your proposals and, instead of a constructive discussion, you verbally lash out in order to 'crush' her and prove how strong you are – accepting some of her criticisms would prove you're a wimp. If you are unassertive and admire someone else's frequent displays of anger because it suggests they have the strength of character that you lack, think again: both of you are suffering from low self-esteem.

Misconceptions about assertiveness

Assertion training is a popular method for gaining greater self-confidence and control over your life and thereby reducing or removing previous feelings of helplessness and hopelessness. As Beck *et al.* point out, assertion is 'an effective antidote to depression' (1979: 83). However, you may misconstrue the role of assertion in your life and thereby subscribe to some of the following ideas.

Acting assertively means that you automatically get what you want

By acting assertively, you may get what you want, but there's no guarantee. Other people may be indifferent or hostile to the declaration of your rights as they may see them as an infringement or negation of their own rights (for example, 'Look, if I turn my music down because it's too loud for you, then I won't be able to enjoy it. So get lost'). In this situation, compromise is not possible (for example, you may have to get the police or local council to enforce your 'right to a quiet life'). Therefore, be realistic about the limits of your newly acquired assertiveness, otherwise you can quickly slip into anger and resentment when people do not respond in the hoped-for way.

Having become assertive, you must act in this manner all the time

Being assertive also means being prudent: undesirable consequences may be avoided if you remain silent or take a low-key approach in certain situations (for example, going to your partner's parents for Sunday dinner in order to avoid a prolonged row if you refuse). Therefore, in some situations it pays to keep quiet. Assertiveness is one option among others and not an automatic reflex in every situation where you feel thwarted or challenged in some way. Being continually 'rights conscious' can lead to the exasperation of your colleagues, partner or friends and result in what Robb calls an 'assertive backlash' as individuals 'find themselves fired, divorced or otherwise disenfranchised' for speaking up (1992: 265). One vision of hell may be living or working with people who will not be denied on any issue.

Being assertive will make people respect or like you (Ellis, 1979)

In fact, domestic, social and work relationships may become increasingly fraught as you begin to assert yourself, (for example, 'It's about time I got some things off my chest') and may even end in rejection (for example, 'I thought she would respect me more, not leave me'). Instead of an anticipated greater interpersonal closeness, others pull back and maintain a wary distance.

Being assertive always equals strength

From this perspective, unassertiveness always equals weakness and therefore you become compulsively assertive to avoid being perceived as weak or inferior by others (for example, 'I never back down in an argument'). Ironically, you're displaying weakness by not allowing yourself to choose when assertion is the best option in a particular situation because you're overly worried about the opinions of others – you're a slave to your perceived public image and if you were to conduct a survey among friends and colleagues, we doubt if they would all agree in their assessment of your image as strong, for example, 'He seems to me obsessed with winning every argument to prove something or other. He comes across as unstable and insecure.'

Being assertive makes you a good person

Assertiveness will probably help you to become adept at getting more of what you want and less of what you don't want; what it will not do is to make you an intrinsically good, better or superior person. Basing your self-worth on a particular behaviour can quickly lead to self-depreciation when you lapse into unassertiveness or find assertiveness 'isn't working' (for example, 'Why aren't people listening to me? It must mean I'm no good again').

Being assertive will solve all your problems

It will undoubtedly help towards solving some of your problems but is certainly not a cure-all. As one person said to me (MN) in a disillusioned tone, 'I thought going on an assertiveness course would transform my life and my problems.' In addition to assertiveness, we would suggest, inter alia, that learning problem-solving skills and developing resilience to cope with adversity (see Chapter 8) are also important.

Blocks to assertiveness

What stops you from being assertive? Hauck (1981b) advances five fears:

1. Fear of injury – for example, physical violence may be threatened or unleashed in order to keep you in thrall such as being trapped in an abusive relationship.
2. Fear of failure – for example, not starting one's own business because it could go all wrong and having to endure the catastrophic consequences that would follow.
3. Fear of hurting other people's feelings – for example, 'If I tell him that he doesn't satisfy me in bed, I will humiliate him, crush him. I'd feel very guilty for doing that to him.'
4. Fear of rejection – for example, continually trying to please others because you believe that not having their love or approval would be devastating, for instance 'I couldn't cope without her love.'
5. Fear of financial insecurity – for example, you stay in a boring job because you're worried about financial instability and potential hardship if you leave it.

Trower *et al.* (2011) suggest:

1. Damning anger – your style of thinking leads you to damn others for frustrating you in some way. Your intention is to hurt or insult others in your interactions with them rather than focusing on trying to get what you want. For example, 'You're a lazy bastard' as opposed to 'I would like to discuss with you a more equal distribution of work around the house'.
2. Guilt – you believe it's wrong to try and fulfil your own wishes because you may equate this with selfishness or, alternatively, you doubt whether you have or deserve any personal rights because you're not worthy enough.

Gilbert (2000) identifies:

1. Fear of counter-attack – when you've made your complaints, you fear being overwhelmed by the other person's response so that you become tongue-tied and blush, your mind goes blank, your words come out in a jumbled fashion, and you end up feeling ashamed or humiliated. In essence, you will come off worst in any encounter.
2. Loss of control – assertion can involve high physiological arousal which might lead to unrestrained behaviour such as shouting obscenities at your partner.
3. Self-blame – you blame yourself for causing problems or conflict when the responsibility for such problems lies with others (for

example, 'It's my fault that my husband hits me. I should stay quiet when he's in a foul mood').

4. Positive self and competitiveness – you view lack of assertiveness as having positive qualities of being good and caring; assertiveness is seen as selfish and pushy: 'To become more assertive threatens becoming similar to people they do not like, and losing a certain satisfaction with self that they are nicer than other people' (Gilbert, 2000: 158).

Lange and Jakubowski (1976) offer another major, but more obvious, reason for unassertiveness: you don't know how to act assertively because of a lack of role models or opportunities to acquire such skills. We would also include: cultural, philosophical and religious beliefs which, for example, emphasise deference, stoicism or self-denial; previous experiences in trying to be assertive which turned out badly for you so that you're reluctant to try again; and unassertiveness being perceived as innate, that is, a fixed part of your personality.

Emotional and behavioural aspects of assertiveness training

The first task is to identify areas of interpersonal difficulty in your life, establish goals for change and then undertake an assessment of your present functioning in those areas. As we have pointed out elsewhere in this book (see Chapter 2 for example), you cannot usually engage in behavioural skills acquisition while emotionally upset. Therefore, you will need to determine if there are emotional blocks to learning assertiveness such as anxiety. In addition, there may be other emotions to contend with. For example, you feel ashamed of and angry with yourself for your perceived weakness in not challenging a friend when she doesn't repay a loan; unable to contain your frustration any longer, you verbally lash out at her, then feel guilty about your angry outburst: 'I shouldn't have lost my temper with her. I'm bad for behaving like that.' You return to your unassertive state, fearing to speak up again in case you unleash the same unnerving roller coaster of emotions but still mired in dissatisfaction with your passivity.

Let's now look at these emotional blocks in turn. First, your anxiety. You are worried that your friend will become angry when you ask her for your money back and reject you, which you will evaluate as 'unbearable'. Is real friendship based on exploitation? You believe that loss of her friendship is unbearable only because you label it that way. If you saw her rejection of you as unpleasant but bearable, this could motivate you to persist in asking for your money back as well as reviewing all your current friendships to decide which are worth preserving and which need to be terminated.

Second, your shame. Not challenging your friend to repay the loan indicates intrapersonal (internal) difficulties that need to be addressed, not self-denigration for being weak. If you see yourself as weak, how will this self-image help you to gain the confidence and strength to be assertive?

Third, your guilt. Your angry outburst confirms your status as a fallible (imperfect) human being, not a bad one. The accumulated frustrations of being unassertive often erupt into anger. This is understandable, but it's better to address your frustrations with others earlier in the sequence of events instead of letting them fester and eventually explode.

Once your emotional difficulties have been tackled, you can then focus on the behavioural skills you need to acquire. It should always be borne in mind that once the emotional problems have improved, your dormant assertiveness may, so to speak, release itself spontaneously.

The main behavioural methods in assertiveness coaching are role play, modelling and rehearsal before enactment in real-life situations. Role play involves a person playing himself first and then switching roles to play the other person in the problem situation; I (MN) would play both roles alternately with the client watching me; then it would be his turn to play both roles. Role playing enables the client to practise his desired behaviour as well as attempt to understand the other person's reactions to such behaviour. Role play also provides further information about the cognitive, emotive and behavioural difficulties in being assertive, for example, the person makes poor eye contact because he believes 'I can't stand the way she looks at me with such contempt'. After role play, I debrief the client in order to deal with any issues that may have arisen from the exercise (for example, the person says 'I can't stay focused on the issue, I get too emotional').

Modelling is used by me to demonstrate to the person how to act assertively and then he practises such behaviour himself. He's not expected to reproduce my behaviour but aims to improve his own interpersonal style in a way that's realistic for him. The person can also be encouraged to observe other role models, for example, work colleagues, friends.

The rehearsal of, and coaching in, the new behaviour pays attention to its verbal and non-verbal aspects. Verbal behaviour includes direct, clear and concise statements using 'I' language and avoids personal abuse, condemnation or being too apologetic. With regard to the non-return of the money, you could say: 'I feel annoyed that you're reluctant to return the money I lent you. Please explain the reasons for the delay and provide a date when the money will be returned. I don't want this incident to jeopardise our friendship.' When being assertive with individuals who are oversensitive, we recommend you use an 'assertive sandwich' because you sandwich what you have to say between two slices of affirmation, for example, 'I always look forward to your phone calls but please don't phone me after midnight. Any other time during the evening will be great to talk to you.' However, things usually turn out better in the textbooks than they do in real life, so the person may hear only the affirmations but not the 'sandwich filler' and continue phoning you after midnight. In this case, deliver only the filler and point out the potentially adverse consequences to the relationship if he does not stop.

Non-verbal behaviour includes focusing on body posture, eye contact, facial expressions, use of gestures, voice level and tone. A clear verbal statement can be undermined by non-verbal behaviour (for example, excessive blinking, keep looking away, frequent swallowing) while para-verbal responses (for example, ers, ums) can blunt the impact of what's being said.

A hierarchy of assertion tasks, from simple to difficult, can be constructed to aid the person's desensitisation to the apprehension he normally experiences in certain interpersonal situations. By gradual exposure to fearful situations, his apprehension is eventually reduced with a corresponding increase in his social competence and confidence; between-session assignments in real-life situations provide the crucial feedback on his performance and any modifications to it that may be needed. He can reward himself each time he has carried out an assertion task in order to reinforce his new behaviour.

In your own efforts to be more assertive, you need to be alert to the presence of task-interfering cognitions (thoughts) or TIC (Burns, 1981), for example, 'I'm being assertive but it's not getting me anywhere. This is not working at all.' TIC can be replaced by TOC (task-orientated cognitions), for example, 'I have to keep reminding myself that being assertive doesn't mean that people will always respond in a positive way or agree with my views. Speaking up for myself is the important point.'

Behaving assertively can help to change or influence the way others behave towards you, such as your opinion is now sought whereas before it was ignored. Such external behaviour also produces important internal effects. That is, we are likely to think and feel differently about ourselves as a result of behaving assertively. By letting other people see, through our behaviour, that we expect to be treated as a person of worth we are also likely to affect our own evaluation of ourselves and what we are capable of. (Sheldon, 1995: 203)

Eight steps to healthy self-assertion

Step 1: get the person's attention

Obvious as this may seem, don't make important points while your partner is reading the newspaper or your colleague is working on the computer. Ensure that you have the person's full attention and distractions (for example, the television is on, colleagues are close by) are avoided.

Step 2: describe objectively the other person's behaviour that you have difficulty with

This means you describe the difficulty without personalising it, making accusations or interpretations (for example, 'You deliberately read the paper when you knew I wanted to talk to you. We're growing further apart and you don't care') and stick to the facts (for example, 'I said I wanted to speak to you and you picked up the paper and started reading it'). As well as being objective, make sure your comments are short otherwise the other person might mentally drift off.

Step 3: express constructive feelings

We would suggest that disappointment and annoyance are constructive feelings to express to your partner or colleague while anger, hurt and jealousy would probably undermine your attempts at being assertive (for example, if you're angry, you're likely to unleash your pent-up frustrations, 'We're growing apart and you don't give a damn!'). Use 'I feel' statements to take responsibility for your feelings (for example, 'I feel annoyed that you would rather read the paper than talk to me') instead of 'You make me feel' statements which then place responsibility for your feelings on to the other person. As we have argued throughout this book, our feelings are largely self-created.

Step 4: check your interpretations and invite a response

You described your partner's behaviour objectively at step 2 but what you really want to convey is your interpretation of his behaviour. Interpretations are not facts, so don't frame them as facts (for example, 'You know we're growing apart') and invite a response to encourage a discussion of the issue (for example, 'It seems to me we're growing further apart and you don't appear to care. What do you think about this?).

Step 5: listen to the other person's response and give feedback

Listening means in an open-minded way instead of dismissing your partner's replies as soon as he's given them (for example, 'Do you really expect me to believe that?'). Listen carefully to what he says (for example, 'I suppose I'd rather read the paper because you keep on about this issue. I don't know where you get the idea from that we're growing apart. If we were, I would care') and then offer your feedback. If you're satisfied with the reply, then say so; if you're not satisfied, then express your doubts without attacking the other person (for example, 'I'm not convinced by your reply: it's not just reading the newspaper, you spend so much time doing things that don't include me').

Step 6: state your preferences clearly and specifically

Your preferences (not demands, for example, 'You must do this!') are based on what you want from the other person or to do together and should be stated in a clear and concrete way (for example, 'We don't have to, but I would like us to go out at least once a week'). You can also point out the positive consequences that are likely to occur (for example, 'I really think it will bring us closer together').

Step 7: request agreement from the other person

If your partner agrees to your proposal, then work out the details (for example, 'Wednesday night will be our going out together night'). If your partner disagrees, ask him what changes he's prepared to make. If he's not prepared to make any changes (for example, 'Why should I change because of your problem') and this is a key area of relationship dissatisfaction for you, then you need to consider carefully the pros and cons of staying in the relationship.

Step 8: communicate any relevant information concerning future episodes

This means telling the other person what you'll do if the problem reoccurs (for example, 'If I feel we're drifting apart again, I will bring it to your attention'), ask the other person in what manner he would like you to respond (possible reply: 'Just tell me in a calm way without jumping up and down about it') and ask him what he'll do differently in future to deal with the situation (possible reply: 'Well, if for any reason going out at least once a week starts to fall off, then I will know something is wrong and it will be "state of the relationship" time again').

Coaching example

Carol was a 30-year-old woman who said she felt trapped in a relationship that she desperately wanted to leave. She described her partner as 'a heavy drinker, he's got no ambition, he's no fun to be with any more, and he spends most of his time stuck in front of the telly'. She said she had tried everything to encourage him to change but to no avail. I (MN) asked her what kept her trapped in the relationship:

CAROL: Well, he's always saying that if I 'abandon' him – that's the word he likes to use – he'll fall apart and drink himself to death and it will be all my doing.

MICHAEL: Do you agree with that?

CAROL: *(sighs deeply)* Well, yes and no. I can't help feeling that I would be responsible in some way but another part of me says that he's the one in charge of his life, not me, so I should pack up and leave.

MICHAEL: But as you don't pack up and leave, does that mean you remain convinced that it would be your fault if he drank himself to death?

CAROL: I suppose I do feel much more strongly it would be my fault rather than his. It's this guilt that he makes me feel that keeps me trapped. He says that if I walk out on him I'll make him feel worthless and his life won't be worth living.

MICHAEL: And again, do you agree with that?

CAROL: Hmm. Well, he's not going to think like that unless I leave him, is he? Also his parents would blame me if anything happened to him. They've called me 'selfish' for thinking about leaving him.

MICHAEL: So you would make him think these thoughts about himself if you left and he makes you feel guilty if you left. On top of all this, his parents point the finger at you as well.

CAROL: And before you ask me . . . yes, part of me does think I'm selfish. It's a big mess, isn't it?

MICHAEL: Well, let's do some coaching in the cognitive dynamics of guilt. For a start, shall we take a closer look at this issue of who is actually responsible for thinking this or feeling that? You might be surprised with what we come up with.

CAROL: Okay, if it will help me to get away from him.

On the whiteboard in my office, I demonstrated the ABC model of emotional upset as it related to Carol's guilt:

A – activating event: imagining her partner's rapid decline and death after her departure
B – beliefs and thoughts: 'I shouldn't have left him, but as I did it's my fault he died. I'm a terrible person for causing his death.'
C – consequences (emotional): intense guilt

Carol was shown that her guilt (C) was largely self-created (that is, the principle of emotional responsibility) by her beliefs and thoughts (B) about the consequences of leaving her partner (A) – in the dynamics of guilt, an act of commission that would bring harm to another. Both the act and the self are condemned by the individual.

The principle of emotional responsibility applied equally to Carol's partner. Her departure may have triggered potentially self-destructive thoughts and feelings in him but these were owned by him, not 'put there' by her. This disputing (D) or questioning of her guilt-producing ideas and apportioning of responsibility in the relationship provided the breakthrough for Carol: if she had the power to destroy him by her departure, why did she not have the same power to revive the relationship or make him behave differently? 'Obviously looking at it now in a more objective way, I don't have this power over him and he doesn't have the power to make me feel guilty unless I let him, which I'm not going to do any more.' Through developing an effective (E) guilt-removing outlook, she was now able to move closer to the final step of leaving:

CAROL: I feel very apprehensive about telling him because he'll get angry, then he'll feel sorry for himself, then the usual threats about drinking himself to death. Then he'll say he will really change this time. He usually gets on the phone to his parents and they come round to persuade me to give him another chance. After all that pressure, I always gave in. This time I don't want to give in and I certainly don't want to sneak out of the relationship like a thief in the night.

MICHAEL: Well, I can teach you some skills in assertiveness to handle this pressure and carry through the decision that you've made.

The principal behavioural method employed was role play where I played the partner and engaged in emotional blackmail to try and change Carol's decision. Initially, she became angry and hurled insults at her 'partner' for past and present hurts; at other times, she became tearful while giving her 'leaving speech' (as she called it). She said she wanted to present her leaving speech 'in a calm, firm and controlled manner and leave with my head held high': 'This relationship ended some years ago for me but I was unable to leave because I allowed myself to be trapped by your emotional blackmail. This is no longer the case and I will be leaving in the morning.'

Digital voice recordings of the sessions were made so Carol could monitor her verbal performance and a full-length mirror was used so she could practise making her verbal and non-verbal behaviour congruent (filming the rehearsal would be even better so she could evaluate her performance). After several sessions of rehearsing her new behaviour, she delivered her leaving speech to her partner – his parents were also there – and left the relationship.

At a three-month follow-up session, she said that 'leaving him has really changed my life for the better in so many ways'. Though she expressed no ill-will towards her former partner, she had no interest in or curiosity about his current whereabouts or well-being: 'There's no point in him being out of my life physically if I still let him live with me mentally.'

Conclusion

As we have shown in this chapter, assertiveness is not always easy to teach as you can have emotional blocks that prevent or hinder the learning and application of behavioural skills; also, you may harbour misconceptions about becoming assertive that promise more than can be delivered. When misconceptions have been corrected, blocks removed and skills learnt, the act of assertion allows you to make a stand when it matters: 'That is, when they [or you] are too often called upon to deny their true feelings or to bear more than their fair share of the emotional costs of living in harmony with other people' (Sheldon, 1995: 210).

Chapter 8

Developing resilience

Introduction

Why is it that one person can withstand multiple crises while another person crumbles in the face of the slightest misfortune? This kind of example is usually the starting point for an investigation into resilience. There isn't such a clear-cut division between the resilient and non-resilient, however: the first person may soon reach his breaking point if he has yet more crises to deal with while the second person may eventually find within herself unexpected strengths to cope with adversity. As research shows, resilience is not a fixed characteristic where the person is resilient at all times under all circumstances; the level of resilience demonstrated varies depending upon the circumstances such as facing adversity alone or with support (Masten and O'Dougherty Wright, 2010). So, what is resilience? We would define it as marshalling your resources to cope with tough times and emerging from them sometimes stronger, wiser, more capable yet this empowering self-assessment can sometimes be offset with a sober accounting of the personal costs of victory (as you will see in some of the stories we present). At the heart of resilience is your attitude to how you cope with what befalls you in life:

> Our research has demonstrated that the number-one roadblock to resilience is not genetics, not childhood experiences, not a lack of opportunity or wealth. The principal obstacle to tapping into our inner strength lies with our cognitive [thinking] style – ways of looking at the world and interpreting events that every one of us develops from childhood.
>
> (Reivich and Shatté, 2002: 11)

Many things happen in life that we have no control over, but our attitudes and judgements are within our control and therefore can be changed if we so choose. Your attitude to misfortune could include taking refuge in drink and drugs, putting your head in the sand, giving up, complaining to anyone who'll listen, seeing it through to the end with or without support; and you can go through a variety of responses (for example, anger, despair and determination) as you push yourself to get through dark times. Some writers and researchers aver that surviving adversity might fall short of a resilient outcome if the person is mired in bitterness, self-pity and victimhood; so it's not survival in itself that's the focus of resilience research but the question: has there been an adaptive process of recovery, that is, surviving and thriving? Also, it's not as easy as it may seem to say who is demonstrating resilient behaviour in times of misfortune: a snapshot of a particular moment in the struggle can give the wrong impression of who will make it in the longer term and who won't. I (MN) worked as a therapist in the NHS for twenty years and I treated many clients who led chaotic, self-destructive lives. Some died, some seemed forever trapped in despair, and some pulled through. If I'd been a betting man I would have lost a lot of money predicting who would and who wouldn't make it to a brighter future. The moral here is don't give up on people or assume the worst just because they're not bouncing back from adversity; self-righting (that is, regaining or finding purpose and direction in life) is sometimes a long process.

Bouncing back or coming back?

What we think is unhelpful in discussing resilience is the popular idea of bouncing back from adversity which reminds me (MN) of a childhood toy I had: a blow-up, chest-high figure of Yogi Bear which, when punched, fell to the floor but sprang back immediately to the upright position. Bouncing back suggests a rapid and effortless return from adversity with barely a hair out of place, an enviable sangfroid (saying to someone who has been off sick for six months and is on a graduated return to work programme, 'Good to see you bouncing back' is nothing of the sort). Bouncing back might be the ideal that some wish to aspire to but if not achieved at times of crisis may trigger self-depreciation (seeing oneself as inadequate) because the person is trapped within this narrow, one speed (bouncing) vision of resilience. If the person can spring back so effortlessly, was it a genuine adversity she actually experienced? Is staying late at work for several days in a row just as much of an adversity as being caught up in a bomb blast?

Another unhelpful idea about resilience is that survival of hard times has tempered the steel of your character and it will never break, you're now constitutionally unbreakable. No matter how robust you've become by overcoming the odds, you still remain vulnerable to coping poorly with future adverse events; no one has an absolute resistance to adversity. In his study of the psychological effects of war on soldiers, *The Anatomy of Courage* (1945/2007), Lord Moran (Charles Wilson) famously likened courage to capital, not continuing income: whatever the amount in any individual soldier's account, it will eventually be spent: 'When their capital was done, they were finished' (2007: 70).

This belief of invulnerability was exemplified by a tough and resourceful manager I (MN) was coaching who was involved in a car accident and suffered some cuts and bruises as well as shock. The real shock for him was that he needed a week off work to recover. He had a normal human response to the accident but dismissed it contemptuously as 'being pathetic' and couldn't understand why he wasn't back at his desk the next day (or even that afternoon!). He thought he was stress resistant – no adverse event could weaken or undermine his fortitude. Initially, he made matters worse for himself by refusing to learn some important lessons from the discrepancy between his actual response to the accident and the ideal one he demanded of himself; eventually, he reformulated his view of resilience in more realistic terms: 'Still strong and capable, but vulnerable at times' (he used to think that only losers showed vulnerability). He also provided more support to those of his colleagues he had previously dismissed as losers when they complained about their heavy workloads or missed performance targets.

Some clients like to say to us: 'Whatever doesn't kill me makes me stronger' and see this as a self-evident truth. Such maxims – this one from the nineteenth century German philosopher Friedrich Nietzsche – need to be examined to determine if there is any substance or value to them. What doesn't kill you can leave you weakened or shattered as the writer Christopher Hitchens discovered:

> I have now lost almost a third of my body mass since the cancer was diagnosed: it may not kill me, but the atrophy of muscle makes it harder to take even the simple exercises without which I'll become more enfeebled still . . . One finds that every passing day represents more and more relentlessly subtracted from less and less. In other words, the process both etiolates you and moves you nearer towards death . . . [and though he remained combative towards the cancer] . . . one can dispense with facile maxims that don't live up to their apparent billing.
>
> (2012: 70–2)

On the subject of 'facile maxims', aphorisms, familiar proverbs, quotations and sayings, we encourage you not to let them pass through your mind and out of your mouth unexamined as you might find that some of them, when scrutinised, have little comfort to offer or real wisdom to impart. If you do emerge from adversity a stronger person, it's because of your dogged determination to prevail, not some automatic process of turning lemons into lemonade (adversity into advantage). Also, what kind of strength has emerged from this process? Are you more compassionate to yourself and others because of what you've learnt from your experiences such as demonstrating humility because you're fallible after all and you can't bounce back from every adversity; or seeing others as weak because they struggled unsuccessfully against the odds? With regard to turning adversity into advantage, Haidt (2006), drawing on a large body of research, describes three key findings:

1. Our self-image is changed. Rising to meet the challenge of dark times can tap into unimagined abilities which changes the way you see yourself – for example, from nervous insecurity to steely determination – which then, in turn, changes the way you view handling future difficulties.
2. The nature of our relationships is clarified and enriched. We begin to see who our fair-weather and all-weather friends are. This can be both dispiriting and surprising: dispiriting because some presumed friends are, strangely, no longer visiting or returning your phone calls, but surprising as friends you weren't particularly close to, or not too keen on in some cases, provide invaluable support during your term of trial. As well as sifting through friendships, struggling with adversity helps to strengthen family bonds and draws you closer together.
3. Our priorities in life are altered. It's as if your new perspective following the trauma has cut a swathe through your life removing anything from it that is seen as unimportant. Your brush with death has made you acutely aware that time is precious and you don't want to waste this irreplaceable resource.

Another point to consider with the bouncing back image is this: does your life return to exactly the same state it was before the adversity? As new meaning and purpose has emerged from overcoming the adversity – the transformational component we might call it – some previous beliefs and behaviours will probably be changed, friendships revisited, values revised, so it's very unlikely that your life would return unchanged to its pre-adversity state. And for this new meaning to emerge, considerable time might be needed to process emotionally-charged material resulting from the adversity (for example, the unexpected death of a family member). Bouncing back suggests little time would be allowed for this process.

For all the above reasons, we prefer the term coming back to bouncing back because it allows for multiple pathways and speeds in responding to adversity (Neenan, 2009). For example, responding quickly to a time-limited (48 hours) crisis at work; or working out over the longer term how to live with chronic pain while not allowing it to become the central focus of your life. Resilient responding to events is individually based as there is no prescriptive way for people to be resilient: they can assemble their own resilience-building strategies depending on their personality styles, ages, individual strengths, cultural differences – customised resilience. For example, one person prefers to sort out her difficulties alone while another person goes to his friends for support and advice. However, don't become stuck in one problem-solving approach as it might indicate the presence of unhelpful beliefs, for example, 'I can't ask for help as it's a sign of weakness.' Finally, the research shows that everyone has the capacity to become resilient, it's not the innate ability of a chosen few; therefore, resilience is ordinary, not extraordinary (Grotberg, 2001; Southwick and Charney, 2012).

Emotion and behaviour in resilience

Resilience can be misconstrued as noble forbearance in the face of pain and suffering: showing emotion is weakness of character. Resilience is actually about managing emotions, not suppressing them. If there appears to be no obvious emotion, this might indicate incomplete processing of the experience and is likely to perpetuate poor, not resilient, responding to future events. In our work with business people, some of the usual phrases they like to use about adverse workplace events are 'suck it up', 'moving forward', 'moving to the next level' and 'putting processes in place'. It's as if by saying the words, the problems have been resolved. An executive said she 'sucked it up and moved on' when her boss 'tore into me at a meeting accusing me of failures that really belonged to some other people around the table'. After the meeting, people commented on her enviable coolness under fire. A week later her personal assistant (PA) made a scheduling error in her appointments diary and 'I tore into her with a ferocity that shocked me and reduced her to tears. When I calmed down I profusely apologised and told her the real story: I was still seething with anger at how I'd been treated at the meeting and she got the full force of it. I hadn't sucked it up at all, it had been festering away. Luckily my PA forgave me. I promised never to behave like that again and took her out to an expensive restaurant. Over the weekend I had a long conversation with a close friend and worked out how I was going to react, professionally but firmly, if my boss treats me like that again.' The only way you can have an unemotional response to an event is if you truly don't care what has happened to you because the event has absolutely no significance for you. By definition, adversities are negative events which are likely to trigger negative emotions in you for the obvious reason that you didn't want these unpleasant events to occur; so these emotions will need to be worked through in order to find adaptive responses to unpleasant events and then 'sucking it up and moving forward' will have some genuine meaning instead of the manufactured one to serve your self image.

You might believe that in your struggle to overcome adversity, you have to succeed at every step along the way. This is a huge burden to carry and gives a false picture of resilient behaviour. Behaviour can be divided into action tendencies (that is, how you may or may not act in a situation) and completed actions (that is, what you actually did in that situation). For example, you want to complete a marathon which requires long and hard training; however, the majority of your action tendencies (for example, putting the alarm on to get up for an early morning run or resolving to go for a run when you get home from work) are not converted into completed actions (you went for a run) and the idea of completing a marathon fades away. Acting resiliently can be seen as carrying out a majority of actions to completion (for example, 80 per cent of the time) and engaging in a minority of action tendencies that don't translate into completed productive actions (for example, 20 per cent of the time). So resilient behaviour involves acting non-resiliently at times, but do ensure that your resilience balance sheet shows more assets (productive behaviours) than liabilities (non-productive behaviours). For example, I (WD) struggle with my weight and have a tendency to snack between meals which if left unchecked would result in putting on weight. Whenever I'm at a party and waiters bring around canapés, the following dialogue often ensues:

WAITER: Would you like a canapé?
WINDY: Yes, but I'm not going to have one.

My response shows that I have an action tendency towards taking a canapé based on my desire (I like canapés and if I could eat them without putting on weight, raising my blood pressure and cholesterol levels, then I would) but my completed action is not to have one and I move away from the waiter. It's important to bear in mind this distinction between action tendencies and completed actions as it's the latter actions that will help you to achieve your goal of greater psychological robustness.

Blocks to developing resilience

These blocks are unhelpful ideas that keep people trapped in non-resilient ways of responding to life's vicissitudes.

1. 'It's not my fault. I'm a victim.' This means feeling helpless in the face of events, continually blaming others for your misfortunes and not taking responsibility for effecting constructive change in your life. Helplessness is an assumption, not a fact, because it's based on the view that there is nothing you can do to change. There's usually a range of options in dealing with each difficulty that we face and to deny this (for example, 'You're wrong. There's no way forward!') doesn't stop these options from existing – if you widen your perspective you're likely to see them. With regard to blame and responsibility, even if others did cause or contribute to your misfortunes, the problem is still yours to solve whether or not you get assistance from them. For example, if your car burst into flames after being hit by a lorry, would you refuse to rescue yourself because you didn't cause the crash and insist that the lorry driver pull you out of the burning wreckage or would you make a determined effort to save yourself irrespective of his behaviour?

2   'I'll never get over it.' The 'it' may be a traumatic event, unhappy childhood or any stressful episode the person believes destroyed her life, sense of security or identity. Can a shattered Humpty-Dumpty ever be put back together? Flach (2004) argues that 'falling apart' in the face of significant stress is part of the resilience response as during this period of disruption new ways of responding to life events can be developed so that the pieces of ourselves can be reassembled in a different and sturdier way. Therefore, no experience is wasted, including a breakdown, in terms of what it can teach us about our adaptive potential to learn from our experiences.

3. 'I'm a failure. There's no point in trying to change.' Such self-devaluation keeps the person in a state of demoralised inertia as he acts in accordance with his self-image – 'This is how I am'. This self-image is not fixed in perpetuity: he can learn to develop a balanced (that is,

looking at oneself in the round) and compassionate view of himself and thereby refrain from harmful self-judgements. Decoupling the behaviour from the self can lead to a new outlook – that one's behaviour will sometimes inevitably fail, but the person never does.

4. 'Why me?' The answer is usually implicit in the question: 'It shouldn't have happened to me. I don't deserve this. I've done nothing wrong or bad.' Her assumption of a just world has been shattered by the traumatic experience. 'Why me?' introspection is unlikely to yield any new or helpful information to tackle her distress (this is our experience in working with clients who have experienced trauma). For what kind of answers would satisfy you? The world is often cruel and arbitrary and makes no distinction between the worthy and unworthy. You don't say 'Why me?' when life is fair, so why should you say it when life is unfair? Searching for answers to 'Why me?' will provide no relief from your suffering (and probably intensify it) and prevent you from processing the trauma in a constructive way.

A radical change of perspective, however, might provide a different and probably unwanted kind of answer. 'Why not me?' states an unpalatable truth: no one is immune from the possibility of experiencing tragedy, trauma or misfortune in life. The late journalist and author, Christopher Hitchens, was diagnosed with oesophageal cancer and said in an American television interview with Anderson Cooper: 'You can't avoid the question ['Why me?'] however stoic you are; you can only bat it away as a silly one as large numbers of people die every day around the world; so to the dumb question "Why me?" the cosmos barely bothers to return the reply: "Why not?"' (2012: 6). The focus should be on what options are available to you to deal with unfortunate events: in Hitchens case, getting the best that modern medicine has to offer in order to try and prolong his life. Endless 'Why me?'-ism will keep you trapped in your misfortune thereby excluding the possibility of recovery from adversity.

5. 'It shouldn't have happened!' This viewpoint encompasses any situation the person feels frustrated about. Denying reality just prolongs and usually exacerbates his current difficulties and frustrations. Like 'Why not me?', 'It should have happened' offers an unexpected perspective: all the conditions were in place at the time for it to have happened. For example, the person was low on petrol and kept passing petrol stations because he was not prepared to queue in his eagerness to get home after a tiring day (his behaviour might have been different if he'd been less tired or forced himself to stop focusing on his

tiredness). To his disbelief, he eventually ran out of petrol, several miles from home. As Edelman (2006: 74) observes: 'Everything that we say and do, including those things that turn out to have negative consequences, happens because all of the factors that were necessary for them to occur were present at that time.' Therefore, he couldn't have acted other than he did because of his thinking at *that* time in *that* situation. So it's time-wasting and unproductive to demand that what undoubtedly happened shouldn't have happened and, instead, turn his attention to learning from the incident in order not to repeat his mistake, for example, get petrol on his way to work.

Attitude: the heart of resilience

We said earlier that your attitude is of central importance when you're facing adversity. Attitude in action can be seen in the following examples of remarkable resilience in extreme circumstances.

A modern day Epictetus

Epictetus (c. AD 55–135), a freed slave, was a Stoic philosopher who along with other Stoics such as Marcus Aurelius and Seneca provided the philosophical foundations of CBT with their view that perturbation (mental unease) is the result of our judgements about events, not of the events themselves (Robertson, 2010). Epictetus's philosophy has had an enormous influence on Western thought and is still with us: 'The more one reads in the literature of self-help, therapy, [coaching], recovery and so forth, the more apparent it becomes how much is owed to this regularly rediscovered author' (Dobbin, 2008: xix).

James Stockdale (1923–2005) was a passionate devotee of Epictetus's doctrines. Stockdale was a navy pilot shot down over North Vietnam in 1965. While drifting down in his parachute towards the ground and facing the prospect of long imprisonment, he whispered to himself: 'I'm leaving the world of technology and entering the world of Epictetus' (1993: 7). Stockdale endured over seven years of captivity including torture and long periods of solitary confinement. He went into captivity with a broken leg and even though it was crudely operated on, he was in pain for several years. Stockdale frequently consoled himself with Epictetus's dictum (he had memorised many of his dictums):

> Lameness is an impediment to the leg but not to the will [Epictetus was lame]; and say this to yourself with regard to everything that

happens. For you will find such things to be an impediment to something else, but not truly to yourself.

(Stockdale, 1993: 11)

His Epictetan outlook informed his style of leadership as the senior commanding officer in the prison. He attributed his ability to endure captivity and return home psychologically intact, but physically debilitated, to Epictetus's teachings. Sherman (2005: 6) saluted Stockdale's Epictetan experiment as 'empowerment in enslavement'. Stockdale was much in demand as a speaker: his central theme was how to prevail when facing adversity, whether in war or peace.

Light in her darkness

Helen Keller (1880–1968) lost her sight and hearing at an early age. She was helped to speak, read and write by a teacher, Annie Sullivan (the 1962 film *The Miracle Worker* starring Anne Bancroft is based on their relationship). Helen grew up to become an author, lecturer and educator of the blind as well as supporting other progressive causes. She was viewed by many people around the world as an inspiring role model in overcoming such seemingly insurmountable handicaps. Though the temptation to succumb to a life of pessimism was great, she resisted it (she said that no pessimist ever opened a new doorway for the human spirit):

Sometimes, it is true, a sense of isolation enfolds me like a cold mist as I sit alone and wait at life's shut gate. Beyond there is light, and music, and sweet companionship; but I may not enter. Fate, silent, pitiless, bars the way . . . but my tongue will not utter the bitter, futile words that rise to my lips, and they fall back into my heart like unshed tears. Silence sits immense upon my soul. Then comes hope with a smile and whispers, "There is joy in self-forgetfulness." So I try to make the light in others' eyes my sun, the music in others' ears my symphony, the smile on others' lips my happiness.

(Keller, 1903/2007: 64–65)

These two extraordinary individuals (and there are a limitless number of others to draw upon) have much to teach us that can be applied to our own lives: principally, that we have the ability to develop an inner freedom from despair and thereby face whatever confronts us in life with courage, determination and dignity.

Resilience is ordinary, not extraordinary

As we mentioned earlier in this chapter, resilience is a common quality, not a rare one. The above examples we would place at the awe-inspiring end of the resilience continuum. Closer to the other end of the continuum is the resilience of everyday life such as taking the children to and from school, holding down a job, looking after pets, caring for an elderly parent. This view might be dismissed by most people as 'simply getting on with it' and see nothing resilient about what they do. However, what would happen to the children, pets, jobs and elderly parents without the person's persistence, dedication and problem-solving skills? Grayling offers a moving portrait of the courage of daily life:

> Ordinary life evokes more extraordinary courage than combat or adventure because both the chances and inevitabilities of life – grief, illness, disappointment, pain, struggle, poverty, loss, terror, heartache: all of them common features of the human condition, and all of them experienced by hundreds of thousands of people every day – demand kinds of endurance and bravery that make clambering up [Mount] Everest seem an easier alternative.
>
> (2002: 21–22)

When companies bring in motivational speakers to fire up the executives they usually hire people who have won Olympic gold medals, sailed round the world or 'clambered up Everest' – individuals who are winners, who have the right stuff. We sometimes suggest to companies, without much interest on their part, that they also hire Mr or Mrs Ordinary as motivational speakers for the following reasons. These athletes, sailors and mountaineers chose to take on these tasks, prepared rigorously for them and generally knew what they were going to face whereas John Smith was totally unprepared for the overwhelming adversity that felled him. He struggled mightily to recover and was eventually able to shape his life into something resembling normality. This is a different kind of courage and a more interesting and inspiring one we believe. Next time you applaud the courage and determination of a great athlete, also spare a thought for people who have to walk miles every day to get clean water and find a few scraps of food to feed their families.

There's no education like adversity

Some people lead relatively uneventful lives – no traumas or tragedies – and their personalities are not cracked open for inspection as usually happens when adversity strikes. To those struck by adversity, the education they receive is usually a favourable one: within those dark, early days of confusion and helplessness they find the will to force their way through to a brighter future and becoming a stronger person in the process. The emphasis is always on a positive outcome: they like what they see about themselves and what they've achieved. This is the sequence of events usually found in the self-help literature which we might, perhaps unfairly, characterise as 'triumphant feel goodism'. The writer Barbara Ehrenreich was diagnosed with breast cancer and investigated what support was on offer in the breast cancer survivor culture and found a kind of tyrannical cheerfulness along with pink ribbons and teddy bears: 'Positive thinking seems to be mandatory in the breast cancer world, to the point that unhappiness requires an apology . . . The cheerfulness of breast cancer culture goes beyond mere absence of anger to what looks, all too often, like a positive embrace of the disease' (2009: 26–7). This 'embrace' usually means believing you've become a better person through fighting and surviving the cancer and, in some cases, the cancer was even seen as a 'gift' to bring about this transformation. Of course, if you try to convince yourself that disease or disability is a 'gift' but don't really believe it, you will make your struggle to cope with infirmity that much harder.

But there's a darker side to this education and the view is not so favourable. For example and to be very dramatic, in your frenzied determination to get a place on a lifeboat as the ship sinks, you knock aside children, old people, and the infirm. You survive, with others, for ten days adrift in the Pacific and the media praise your bravery (without discovering your earlier behaviour which might then change to public revulsion); however, you're ashamed of your initial panic-stricken ruthless behaviour and it remains for you unforgettable and unforgiveable.

Paul Steinberg (1926–1999) turned his mind into a calculator to continually assess the adaptive behaviour required of him to change the odds in his favour in order to survive Auschwitz. After the war he became a businessman and hardly a day passed without him feeling glad that he'd survived and yet

> There remains a critical point that seems to torment me in particular . . . It's the question of dignity, my dignity as a human being . . . I believe I've led an upright life, one perhaps best described as honest. But I have never, ever, been able to break free of my former existence. I lived and am still living in humiliation, I have never managed to wipe my image clean. I am still the passive witness of Philippe's

death, the person who slapped the old Jew, the boy hiding out in the latrines, the toady who fawned on brutes and murderers to make sure of his extra helpings of soup.

(2001: 162).

In his own defence, Steinberg said that ideal behaviour under such appalling circumstances was out of reach. Another Auschwitz inmate, psychiatrist Viktor Frankl (1905–1997) saw that the worst of circumstances could bring out the best in human nature such as some prisoners giving away their last piece of bread to help others; other prisoners preyed on the weak and sick. Witnessing the best and the worst in human behaviour, he realised that both these potential behaviours reside in us all and which one is acted upon depends on the decisions we make, not the conditions we find ourselves in ('decisions but not on conditions', as he pithily remarked [1985: 157]).

In concluding this section, we note that the education one receives from tackling adversity can be both rewarding and unsettling rather than automatically assuming it to be character building and life affirming.

Attributes associated with resilience

Writers on resilience invariably offer their list of attributes comprising resilience. This is our list of the key attributes informing a resilient outlook (these attributes are also discussed in other chapters as they're essential in developing personal effectiveness across the lifespan).

- High frustration tolerance – the ability to endure in times of upheaval without continually complaining how difficult the struggle is or lapsing into self-pity every time a new setback is encountered.
- Keeping things in perspective – not jumping to catastrophic or gloomy conclusions when difficulties are experienced but, instead, appraising events in a calm and measured way that enables you to see what aspects of the situation you can influence and which aspects you cannot.
- Self-acceptance – accepting yourself for the emotional conflicts (for example, 'Why me?' despair alternating with 'Get on with it' grit) and faltering behavioural progress that are part of tackling adversity instead of berating yourself for not rising immediately to the challenge of adversity and overcoming it with faultless determination (this might be a perfectionist's view of what resilience means).

- Adaptability – the ability to think and act flexibly in the face of changing and challenging circumstances.
- Support from others – asking for or accepting support. Resilience is not developed in social isolation and, extending this point, positive relationships are seen as a key protective factor across the lifespan when tough times arrive (Masten and O'Dougherty Wright, 2010).
- Self-control – regulating your emotions and behaviour in order to stay focused within stressful situations and displaying consistent behaviour across situations (so you don't appear to others as unpredictable); keeping a balance between your short- and longer-term goals so you don't overly focus on the former at the expense of the latter, for example, too much partying and little studying lead to poor exam results. As Pinker observes: 'Contrary to the conventional wisdom that says that people with too much self-control are uptight, repressed, neurotic, bottled up, wound up . . . the [research] team found that the more self-control people have, the better their lives are' (2011: 599).
- Curiosity – you like trying things out, asking questions, making discoveries to increase your understanding of the world around you.
- Self-belief – within reason, you have the ability to take your life in the direction you want it to go. Self-belief is coupled with self-control in order to do this.
- Seeking meaning – no matter what difficulties occur in your life, meaning can be extracted from them such as struggling successfully against the odds showed you had 'grit in your soul' which you wouldn't have discovered if you could take every setback in your stride.
- Humour – finding light moments in dark times and, more generally, not taking oneself too seriously.
- Problem-solving skills – identifying and removing internal blocks to change and executing successfully goal-directed action plans (emotional and practical problem-solving).
- Mindfulness – acknowledging the presence of unhealthy negative thoughts and feelings without getting entangled in them; going forward despite their existence.

The above attributes are interdependent and therefore it's difficult to determine which ones are primary in order for the other ones to develop. For example, do problem-solving skills develop because you have the self-control to learn them or is self-control established once you have the self-belief that you're largely in control of your life and can achieve what you want? We would liken this discussion to the question of the chicken and egg: which one came first? Also, as Flach (2004) remarks, there's not a perfectly maintained balance amongst these qualities; rather, a changing emphasis on some qualities more than others at different times, for example, you may be admirably self-disciplined but inclined to let social support recede when it would be helpful to make use of it; you're very curious about trying new experiences but usually avoid those ones where you might be criticised or rejected thereby only half-heartedly attempting to internalise self-acceptance.

Making yourself more resilient

You don't have to 'invite' adversity into your life in order to develop greater resilience (for example, deliberately leave your job to see how you cope with unemployment). What you can do is choose to tackle the difficult or unpleasant situations you're avoiding. A difficult or unpleasant situation is a dictionary definition of adversity, so adversities are already in your life waiting to be faced. How does facing them help you? You raise your threshold, sometimes significantly so, for dealing with frustrations and tolerating discomfort which helps to prepare you for the inevitable and unchosen adversities that lie ahead. This 'discomfort practice' helps you to see that you're stronger than you think. As Irvine (2009: 112) remarks: 'If all we know [or seek] is comfort, we might be traumatized when we are forced to experience pain or discomfort, as we someday almost surely will.' Also, when you start to deal with these situations, you can't be sure of the outcome, for example, pleasantly surprised or more of a curate's egg. (For other ways to improve your level of resilience see Meichenbaum [2012] and Robertson [2012]).

Roger couldn't be bothered with anything dull or boring such as clearing out the spare room and garage; the garden was overgrown and his office was a mess . . . the list goes on. When Roger came to coaching he decided he needed to 'be bothered' and embarked on a programme of immersing himself in all the avoided tasks: reluctantly, angrily but forcefully pushing himself to complete them with unproductive action tendencies (task avoidance) kept to a minimum. The biggest and final task was moving house which his wife had been desperate to do for a long time. Roger had always claimed he was happy where he was but finally admitted to the real reason: his fear of the huge discomfort and upheaval it would cause. Moving house could have been a major source of stress (as rated on life events questionnaires) but, instead, went relatively smoothly with his new be-bothered outlook.

Coaching example

Nancy avoided interpersonal conflict whenever possible. She didn't like to experience 'bad atmospheres' or 'people thinking badly of me'. If she couldn't escape from conflict, then she felt anxious, became tongue-tied and tried to placate the other person by admitting she was in the wrong. Nancy's motto was 'anything for a quiet life' but internally she led a very unquiet life as she was deeply critical of her passivity and cowardice – 'Why can't I fight for myself?' I (MN) explored this question with her.

MICHAEL: Do you think you're worth fighting for?

NANCY: Well, I suppose I am but it's a great effort all the time, so I don't really fight for myself in reality. If people would be nice and reasonable then I'd feel comfortable and things would be easier when I speak up. Yes, I know, life isn't like that all the time.

MICHAEL: It seems that you will only fight for yourself when you feel comfortable and there's no unpleasantness, so what would you need to fight about then?

NANCY: It seems silly when you say it like that. There wouldn't be, would there?

MICHAEL: Look, in essence, is the greater discomfort and unpleasantness changing or staying the same?

NANCY: I've gone over this a lot of times in my mind and staying the same is the worst option and it gets me nowhere.

MICHAEL: Okay. So, there's the useless discomfort, so to speak, of staying the same and with little chance of spontaneous improvement (Nancy nods) and the useful discomfort, so to speak, of forcing yourself to do what you've been avoiding because . . .?

NANCY: Because it will help me to develop some backbone and self-respect and – it's long overdue – to start feeling that I'm more in control of my life. Doing instead of being done to, if you know what I mean.

MICHAEL: I do. This feeling of more control externally will come when you've developed internal control and strength by changing your attitudes to discomfort, conflict and struggle.

NANCY: I hope so, but I can't say I'm looking forward to what I have to do.

As with Roger, Nancy had to embrace what she feared if she was going to make progress: deliberately seek discomfort in order to learn how to tolerate it. As you will see from Nancy's last remark, there was no psyching herself up with exhortations to 'Go for it!' – just a downbeat, reluctant acceptance of what needs to be done. We point this out because you may believe that you have to work yourself up with stirring motivational statements in order to get going yet this method sits uneasily with your way of doing things; so find your own way to get started.

Nancy designed a hierarchy of situations to face where confrontation was expected; these situations ranged from least to most threatening. She started with asking the two boys next door to stop kicking their ball into her garden and putting up with the withering looks from their mother, and then moved on to other situations such as: complaining in restaurants if the food wasn't cooked to her liking; persistently asking her husband to stop dropping his clothes on the floor and put them into the linen basket; and insisting that a work colleague stop speaking to her in a way that Nancy viewed as patronising.

The situation she feared the most was saying no to her sister who expected Nancy to do her bidding and became angry if Nancy demurred (for example, 'She almost orders me to house- and dog-sit when she goes away for the weekend as if I've got nothing else to do which is, unfortunately, true most of the time'). This time Nancy said no and held her ground; her sister stormed off and didn't speak to her again for six months. Working though her hierarchy was anxiety-provoking, often exhausting, she felt physically sick and at times had to fight hard with herself to stay the course. Why didn't she give up?

NANCY: Because I realised, and it always takes quite some time for things to sink in, that staying the way I am is more frightening to me than what I have to do in trying to be a different person, or as different as I can be.

MICHAEL: How do you feel now after coming through this gruelling process?

NANCY: Mixed feelings really. I finally found self-respect by standing up for myself which is all to the good but my world seems to have turned upside down. My marriage is under severe strain and I don't think will last. My husband wants the old Nancy back and feels threatened by the new one. He wasn't much support to me in my struggles. He kept on saying that if it's too much for me, then give up; it would have been nice if just sometimes he could have praised my efforts and given me some encouragement. He kept on telling me to make up with my sister as if it was all my fault. If he does leave me I'm prepared for that as I often felt I was living alone anyway, so I know I will be able to cope. On balance, I'm glad I started it and eventually became bloody-minded about seeing it through to the bitter end, but don't ask me to start celebrating as I don't feel like it. I mean, I feel pleased and sad but also irritated that I didn't do this earlier in my life and wonder why not.

MICHAEL: I won't ask you to celebrate and if it's any consolation to you, you're not the only person to have mixed feelings about the costs involved in getting through such an ordeal.

Like a lot of our clients, Nancy wondered why 'I didn't do this earlier in my life'. In Nancy's case, her attitude of 'anything for a quiet life' which included the avoidance of interpersonal conflict, were key cognitive and behavioural processes maintaining her problems. What you do at any given moment or over a longer period is determined by what you were thinking at the time. Looking back over your life, it's pointless to insist that you should have thought differently about the situation or known what this different thinking was even though you were unaware at the time that you could think differently about it. Let's take this line of reasoning further:

1. Even if you knew there was a better way of dealing with your difficulties, you didn't follow this problem-solving approach.
2 Even if you did start following this approach, you didn't persist with it.
3. Even if you considered seeking professional help because you realised you couldn't do it alone, you didn't follow up on this idea.

Therefore, all the conditions were in place in your life to prevent you dealing effectively with your problems. Retrospectively, you might want to undertake some detective work and try to discover what ideas prevented you from pursuing a different course, for example, 'I don't feel confident enough to do it', 'It's probably a waste of time anyway', 'Maybe things will work themselves out on their own', 'Perhaps I'm trying to convince myself that I'm unhappy when things are not really that bad' and so on.

Conclusion

In this chapter, we've explored the concept of resilience and moved beyond the popular but narrow view of it as bouncing back from adversity. Any genuine adversity would probably preclude much 'bounce'. We prefer the concept of coming back which allows for different speeds and individually-tailored methods of recovery. Your attitude to adversity is central in helping to understand if you're 'struggling well' (O'Connell Higgins, 1994) to find an adaptive response to misfortune or floundering in despair because you believe nothing good can ever come from anything bad. Overcoming adversity won't always provide unalloyed delight: sometimes the outcome will include a sober reckoning of the personal costs of victory.

Chapter 9

Taking risks and making decisions

Introduction

Do you sometimes wish that your life was more exciting and challenging, yet when such opportunities arise you decide not to grab them because the risk of your decision backfiring is, in your mind, too horrible to contemplate? Your watchword is 'better safe than sorry' but your yearnings do not disappear: a continual tension exists between being cautious and wishing to take chances. A risk-averse outlook keeps you disgruntled as you accumulate a lifetime of 'if only . . .' regrets (for example, 'If only I had asked her out when I had the chance but I lost my nerve'; 'If only I had gone on that training course, I could have been higher up the company ladder by now. I didn't want to take the risk of failing the course'). In an echo of Socrates' famous remark that an unexamined life is not worth living, Hauck states that 'the life that has no risk in it is not worth living' (1982b: 57).

We view risk-taking as a sign of psychological health because you want to pursue ambitious goals, are not afraid of setbacks and failures, and want to make your life less self-restricting and more adventurous. It's important to stress that we're not advocating that risk-taking per se is always good for you, but that each risk you take is carefully considered, not recklessly engaged in (for example, you drive your car very fast to impress your partner with your coolness at the wheel; she's terrified and says she could have been killed and promptly dumps you). In this chapter, we will examine why you might see risk-taking as something to be avoided or minimised and decision-making as difficult (even though you take risks and make decisions [for example, motorway driving] every day of your life and these don't present obvious problems for you).

'I can't take the risk'

Risk refers to the chance of an undesirable outcome occurring. The probability of such an outcome 'ranges from practically zero to practically 100 percent' (Wessler and Wessler, 1980: 136). The more feared the outcome, the more probable it is in your mind that it will occur. When you say you cannot take the risk, what you usually mean is: 'I can take the risk but I choose not to' and you choose not to because you believe you will not be able to cope with the consequences of, for example, being rejected or failing. Failure and rejection are probably the two main reasons why people avoid taking risks. Simon would not take the risk of asking Mandy out because she might say no and he believed he would be devastated by her decision. Maxine wanted to leave the NHS and set up in private practice as a therapist but could not accept the risk of 'leaving the nest' and crashing to earth as a failure.

Both Simon and Maxine made the mistake of seeing risk as one-sided (that is, that the feared calamity would occur) rather than also allowing for the possibility that their desires might be fulfilled; in other words, they assumed their negative predictions were accurate. Also, they saw risk as an outcome fixed in aspic (for example, forever crushed by rejection; a lifelong failure) rather than as a continuous process of change, adaptation and learning. As Dryden and Gordon observe:

> Life is neither Utopia nor misery because life isn't static. We cannot halt the flow of change. Change is the only continuity you will ever experience so long as you are alive. But the great plus point is that change brings with it the continuing opportunity to modify and shape change. And through accepting that we are both the products and agents of change in an uncertain world, we are offered the possibility of achieving real personal growth.
>
> (1993: 40–41)

Achieving real personal growth can start with you learning to take the 'horror' (emotional disturbance) out of risk-taking: if you think, for example, that rejection or making a mistake is the ultimate horror, how would you evaluate becoming paralysed from the waist down or being horribly disfigured in a fire? If you saw rejection as no more than an inconvenience, you could keep asking women out, accepting rejection and persisting until you got a 'yes'. Of course, you might fear a positive outcome (for example, receiving a yes means you might not live up to her expectations; getting the promotion means having to prove to the company that you're worthy of their choice) because you're usually looking beyond it to see subsequent failure, for example, losing your job in a departmental reshuffle.

If you don't take risks, then you will have little chance of overcoming your fears. Risk-taking means that you will have some chance of success on some occasions while avoiding risk means hardly any chance at all of success unless it falls into your lap. In our coaching sessions we encourage people to carry out risk-taking exercises. These exercises involve people facing their fears and re-evaluating the outcome such as bearable rather than unbearable, unpleasant but not awful. As Walen *et al.* point out:

> People learn by experience: if they have never experienced failure, they will be unlikely to change their IB's [irrational beliefs] about it and their avoidance of it. Thus, it is difficult to work on the fear of an aversive event unless the client actually experiences it.
>
> (1992: 265)

Coaching example

Frank described himself as a perfectionist. He dreaded making mistakes in those areas of his life where he believed his credibility was at stake such as public speaking ('If I don't perform perfectly, then people will see me as a phoney'). He drove himself relentlessly to perfect his performance: he had to be superbly articulate, answer the most difficult questions with ease and aplomb, know every aspect of his subject, have brilliant rejoinders to anyone who challenged or criticised him, never say 'I don't know' to any question or show a trace of nervousness in his bearing and all the workshop evaluations had to give him the highest scores (it's exhausting just writing this!) Frank exemplified Reinhold Niebuhr's (an American theologian) acute observation that 'perfection has no pity' in the torments people put themselves through to reach standards that are 'beyond reach or reason' (Burns, 1980). Needless to say, Frank's self-worth was tied to the achievement of these standards which he kept falling below as he was ruthless in pinpointing the slightest imperfections in his performance.

Frank said his continual striving to reach these standards is 'grinding me down'. We looked at the advantages and disadvantages of trying to be perfect (*not* being perfect – some clients may try to push the exercise in this direction). The key finding from this exercise was that Frank no longer wanted to pay the high physical and psychological costs of pursuing the holy grail of perfection. While these discussions helped to reinforce his determination to change, the breakthrough was carrying out behavioural experiments in the workshop settings. I (MN) asked him what would happen if he said 'I don't know' to a question to which he actually knew the answer:

FRANK: Why would I do something stupid like that?

MICHAEL: To test out your dire prediction that you would be seen as a phoney, cast out into the wilderness and never asked to do another workshop.

FRANK: Yes, I can see that but I do feel very strongly that these things would happen if I screw up.

MICHAEL: Your feelings are not facts: because you feel very strongly it would be the case you assume it's true. It's called emotional reasoning.

FRANK: It may be emotional reasoning to you but it's very convincing to me.

MICHAEL: Well, there is a way to test this difference of opinion by you carrying out an experiment. What you need to do, if you agree, is to gather accurate information about the outcome and that can only be achieved by taking the risk. What benefits might you gain from this exercise?

FRANK: *(sighs deeply)* I know logically that not being able to answer a question or two is not going to make me a phoney. I don't know any-one who knows their subject one hundred per cent and some of my colleagues keep reminding me that you don't need to be perfect to have a very successful career or the respect of your peers. I suppose I need to prove this to myself, don't I? The pressure I put myself under is often intolerable.

MICHAEL: In what way?

FRANK: Well, I really drive myself incredibly hard to prepare for these presentations, not to mention how irritable I become with every-one; after the presentation, I'm completely drained and I take several days to recover. So easing the pressure would be another benefit.

MICHAEL: But at the moment these benefits are theoretical because . . .?

FRANK: . . . because I haven't done it yet. *(long pause, then sighs)* I'll reluctantly give it a go. My stomach is all in knots just talking about it. Will the experiment make me feel even worse than my pursuit of perfection?

MICHAEL: Another outcome to discuss . . . once you've done the experiment.

When Frank made the momentous confession 'I don't know', there were no shock waves from the audience, the heavens didn't fall, and his psychological meltdown didn't occur; instead the question was answered for him by someone in the audience ('He actually made a good point which I would have overlooked and then it was time for coffee. I didn't feel that anxious about doing the experiment, believe it or not. All in all, the whole experience was something of a damp squib'). Evaluations of his presentation were hardly different from previous ones. He carried out more experiments such as shaking his hand when drinking a glass of water; using some words incorrectly; having to try several marker pens before he found one that was useable; and telling some audiences that he often felt nervous about presenting workshops. No thunderbolts struck him down, workshop evaluations were still high and the work kept coming in.

When carrying out experiments, it's vitally important to remember that you need to be interested in *whatever* the outcome is, not fixated on success or failure; if the experiment has to turn out in a certain way then it's not an experiment – you can't know the outcome before you've conducted the experiment. For example, 'So the experiment is to go to the party and make conversation, instead of keeping quiet like I used to, then people will speak to me, I'll have a good time and make some friends. That seems like a good experiment.' No, the experiment is to go to the party, make conversation and see what happens. Frank's experiments didn't end in any of his feared catastrophes, but how would he have responded if something unnerving had occurred?

MICHAEL: For example, someone in the audience sees your hand shaking while you're drinking a glass of water and says that's a sign of weakness in a workshop presenter.

FRANK: Well, I certainly would go rather wobbly inside having it pointed out so blatantly like that, but after what I've learned in coaching I hope I would have the presence of mind to say that I would have agreed with you in the past but not now. I would explain that I've wasted so much time and effort in life trying and failing to expunge nervousness from my character. Now we co-exist: if it appears, I don't get alarmed, I focus on the workshop and forget about it. I feel more relaxed now running workshops than I ever did.

MICHAEL: Excellent reply.

Frank was more relaxed (but not complacent) about making mistakes while maintaining high, but no longer impossibly high, standards (perfectionists fear that if they relax their standards they will plunge into mediocrity – a living death); and that to be revealed as a phoney would have to mean something much more serious than the failure to answer a question or stumbling over his words: 'If someone in the audience had thought I was a phoney because I couldn't answer a question, then he or she has probably got the same attitudes I used to have,' he said at our last session. He had at last allowed some compassion and flexibility to inform his thinking about his standards and his self-esteem no longer experienced the vertiginous drops of old when his imperfections showed: 'I'm beginning to see the light that my self-worth can remain relatively stable even if I did make a major screw-up at a workshop, but fingers crossed that I don't.' Frank was slowly moving away from rating his worth on the basis of his achievements or failures (the rise and fall of self-esteem) towards a tentative understanding that self-acceptance requires no rating of the self, only of your actions – the psychological stability that this brings if truly internalised is hinted at by Frank.

'I'm not confident enough to try it'

Does confidence come before or after carrying out a difficult activity? You might reply that the logical answer is after. Yet when you're faced with a difficult or new task, you may illogically believe that you should feel confident *before* undertaking it and as the feeling remains elusive, you avoid doing the task (were you confident about taking your first driving lesson; if the answer is probably no, why did you persist with it?) Avoidance doesn't develop confidence. In order to feel confident eventually, you need to start off feeling unconfident as you attempt the activity (for example, learning to dance), acknowledge and analyse your mistakes (for example, missteps), put your new learning into practice, further analysis and practice . . . and so on until you develop performance confidence. In other words, don't put the cart before the horse.

Decision-making

In this section, our focus is on what you might call unhurried decisions and not on those which involve a rapid response (for example, working on the stock market) or require split-second timing (for example, from a racing driver or fighter pilot) which are outside the scope of this chapter.

Decisions, decisions, decisions

Before making a final decision, there are a number of other decisions to consider first. For example, how reliable and up to date is the information you're going to base your decision on? How do you rate the abilities of the person who is helping you to gather and assess the quality of the information? With regard to yourself, are you placing too much emphasis on the first opinions you listened to (primacy effect) or unduly swayed by what the last person told you (recency effect)? If you want an objective observer like a trusted friend or colleague to comment on your proposed decision, do you really want to hear an honest appraisal or hoped-for reassurance that you're making the right decision? You may have six options to choose from, so which ones do you rule out leaving the essential two or three? If your final decision does backfire, do you have another plan of action or are you just praying it turns out successfully?

With so many issues to consider, it may be easy to get bogged down in the technicalities of decision-making and forget the overall purpose of arriving at a decision – to improve your life in some way. So set yourself a realistic timescale for making the decision, estimate the probability of a successful outcome (for example, 70 per cent) and then make and carry out the decision. If the decision does turn out successfully, further decisions will need to be made by you to maintain that success and troubleshoot any foreseeable difficulties that may threaten it. If the decision turns out unfavourably, then more decisions will have to be made in response to this negative outcome. Whatever the circumstances, making decisions is inescapable.

'I wish I was decisive'

Decisiveness is usually seen as a positive attribute: for example, people who can think clearly and quickly in a crisis or, once having made a decision, will see it through to the bitter end. From this viewpoint, decisiveness seems to hinge on one crucial decision and a successful outcome will inevitably follow. In reality, decisions need to be made on a moment-by-moment basis in a crisis (and to correct earlier ones) and moving towards the 'bitter end' needs to be regularly reviewed so that it doesn't become a reality and, instead, just remains a figure of speech. People we see in our coaching sessions who present with difficulties in decision-making are often all-or-nothing thinkers in this area: they see the world as divided into those who are decisive and those who aren't (for example, 'I wish I could be like my colleague, he always knows what to do and doesn't get flustered like me'). We frequently point out that even the most decisive person sometimes vacillates.

On closer examination of their decision-making difficulties, we usually find examples where people have been decisive in their lives (like opting for some coaching sessions) but are currently struggling with certain decisions they have to make. The reasons for their current indecisiveness are then explored. Here are some self-defeating attitudes underpinning indecisiveness.

'I must be sure that I will make the right decision'

You can only be sure that you've made the right decision by evaluating the outcome of your decision and that can only be achieved by making a decision . . . your thoughts go round and round as if they're on a tape loop. You demand a guarantee before you act yet you know no such guarantee is possible or forthcoming (there is one guarantee: if you continue to demand one, you will remain indecisive). The best you can do is to make a decision based on the available information and have a contingency plan ready if the outcome is a negative one. Right or wrong decisions are based on hindsight, not foresight.

'I must be comfortable when I make decisions'

Choosing between alternative decisions that both have advantages can leave you feeling uncomfortable as you realise you will not be able to enjoy the advantages of the non-preferred decision. For example, a friend of mine (MN) had two attractive women chasing him and he could not make up his mind which one to go out with as they both excited him; they got fed up waiting for his decision and eventually lost interest in him. The moral of the story is: it's better to enjoy some advantages than none at all.

Comfort is also a problem when you protest that you cannot make a decision as 'I don't feel right'. If the decision is an especially difficult one (for example, leaving a relationship) you may actually feel increasingly uncomfortable as you delay making the announcement. If there is any comfort to be experienced, this usually comes after the decision is made, not before it.

'I must make the right decision because if I make the wrong one, this proves I am stupid and inadequate'

With this attitude, you put your self-esteem on the line when you make a decision. Even if you make a wrong one, this is hardly conclusive evidence that you're a stupid or inadequate person. If you're making a series of bad decisions, this points to poor decision-making skills and urgent attention is obviously required. As we've pointed out elsewhere in this book, your actions can never describe, define or label you because of your complexity as a fallible human being. If you were truly stupid and inadequate, then every decision you made or anything else you ever did in life could only turn out to be inadequate no matter how much expert help you received. This reading of human behaviour suggests you can't learn from your mistakes or change.

Kathryn Schulz challenges our notions of what it means to be wrong:

> Of all the things we are wrong about, this idea of error might well top the list. It is our meta-mistake: we are wrong about what it means to be wrong. Far from being a sign of intellectual inferiority, the capacity to err is crucial to human cognition . . . wrongness is a vital part of how we learn and change. Thanks to error, we can revise our understandings of ourselves and amend our ideas about the world. Given this centrality to our intellectual and emotional development, error shouldn't be an embarrassment, and cannot be an aberration.
>
> (2010: 5)

Being wrong is part of a scientist's mindset and is how progress is made. Theories are tested and supported, revised or abandoned in the light of evidence from these experiments. Similarly, when you examine and test your thoughts and beliefs you're acting like a personal scientist and results from your experiments can help you to make better decisions, develop more accuracy in your judgements and lead to the acknowledgement that being wrong has led to some welcome improvements in your life.

'I must make the right decision in order not to lose your approval'

The need for approval can be at the heart of indecisiveness, particularly where tough decisions are called for. For example, Peter's business had run into financial trouble and one of his three employees would have to be dismissed in order to cut back on costs. Peter liked his employees and agonised over who it should be ('They've all got mortgages to pay and kids to feed. Whichever one I get rid of will end up hating me and that will bother me a great deal') while the financial costs continued to mount. Peter's decision was eventually made for him as one of them left to seek opportunities elsewhere. Peter's bottom line was the need for approval instead of cutting costs to save his business (Peter said he might even have let his business go to the wall rather than dismiss one of his employees). While the approval of others is desirable, it's not essential to have it and developing a tough-minded attitude will help you to become decisive about unpopular decisions you have to make, for example, 'If he doesn't like me, so be it. I can't allow my business decisions to be based on my poll ratings with the staff.'

Too decisive

Being too decisive usually stems from impulsive decision-making – you act on the spur of the moment instead of thinking through the implications of your proposed decision, and often end up sabotaging your future interests (for example, you lose all your savings on Internet trading in stocks and shares because your friend told you how easy it was to make 'a quick killing'). Impulsive decision-making is often motivated by how you're feeling at that moment, for example, you feel down in the dumps and decide to go on a spending spree to cheer yourself up thereby adding another thousand pounds to your credit card; you feel angry with your boss for cancelling another meeting with you, hurl some abuse at her which leads to you being disciplined. We would suggest that a lot of impulsive decision-making is fuelled by low frustration tolerance, that is, you believe you can't stand the acute discomfort of having to wait, holding your tongue, delaying your pleasures, listening to others' often opposing opinions or thinking things through in a methodical fashion. You may defend your impulsive decision-making style as, for example, 'he who hesitates is lost', 'never pull your punches' or 'go with the moment', but this outlook brings you more poor results than successful ones. Justified caution and pulling punches can rein in your impulsiveness and lead to more considered decision-making.

Decision-making styles

People obviously differ in their decision-making styles (for example, cautious or impulsive) and usually adopt different styles in different situations. Arnold, Cooper and Robertson (1995: 257) list six decision-making styles:

1. Without thought
2. Compliant
3. Logical

4.   Emotional
5.   Intuitive
6.   Hesitant

You might be logical when it comes to work-based decisions (for example, 'We have four options to consider carefully before presenting our decision to the board'), intuitive in judging people (for example, 'I always go on first impressions, what my gut instinct tells me'), compliant with your partner (for example, 'If that's what's going to satisfy you, then let's do it') and emotional with your children (for example, 'I like my children to be happy so it's hard for me to say no to them'), hesitant about a fitness programme (for example, 'I don't know if this is for me: I've got to give up cigarettes, cut down on the booze and fry-ups and will I really be any happier?'), and apply no thought to unimportant decisions (for example, 'Look, I don't care what wine we have with the dinner, so long as it's wet and in a glass').

Some decision-making styles may prove to have more disadvantages than advantages and a change is required, for example, more of your decisions regarding your children's behaviour are logical such as 'What lessons am I teaching them and myself if I never say no to them?' rather than emotional as you want to avoid them growing up as spoiled brats. As well as your decision-making style, your decisions can be influenced by, among other factors, illness, your emotional state and the amount of stress you're under. With regard to stress, faulty decision-making can occur if you have too little stimulation or stress and for that reason you might be inattentive when making a decision; or you may be under great pressure and struggling to cope with it and, consequently, don't carefully appraise the various options with the rigour they require (Quick *et al.*, 2013). Therefore, postpone important decisions if you're psychologically off-balance and look for ways to restore the balance (for example, going for a long walk, putting the phone on silent and enjoying some quiet time, having a swim) so your eventual decision will have less chance of rebounding upon you.

Cost-benefit approach to decision-making

Once you have tackled successfully some of the self-defeating attitudes underpinning poor decision-making, you can then use the cost-benefit analysis forms (see Figure 9.1). There are six steps you need to follow in using these forms (which would be the same steps if you had more than two options).

Advantages/Benefits of Option A

SHORT TERM

For yourself	For other people
1	1
2	2
3	3
4	4
5	5
6	6

LONG TERM

For yourself	For other people
1	1
2	2
3	3
4	4
5	5
6	6

Disadvantages/Costs of Option A

SHORT TERM

For yourself	For other people
1	1
2	2
3	3
4	4
5	5
6	6

LONG TERM

For yourself	For other people
1	1
2	2
3	3
4	4
5	5
6	6

Figure 9.1(a) Cost-benefit analysis form.

Advantages/Benefits of Option B

SHORT TERM

For yourself	For other people
1	1
2	2
3	3
4	4
5	5
6	6

LONG TERM

For yourself	For other people
1	1
2	2
3	3
4	4
5	5
6	6

Disadvantages/Costs of Option B

SHORT TERM

For yourself	For other people
1	1
2	2
3	3
4	4
5	5
6	6

LONG TERM

For yourself	For other people
1	1
2	2
3	3
4	4
5	5
6	6

Figure 9.1(b) (Continued).

1. Describe clearly the two options (A and B) you're going to choose between. Write the option down on each sheet of the cost-benefit form.
2. Take one of the options (for example, option A) and focus on the advantages/benefits of choosing this option both in the short and long term for yourself and others such as family members.
3. Write down the corresponding disadvantages/costs of choosing this option, again in the short and long term for yourself and others.
4. Repeat the advantages/disadvantages analysis for the other option (B).
5. Go away for an hour or two and clear your head before coming back to the forms and reviewing what you've written. Read your responses on each page and ask yourself the following question: on balance, after taking into account the information you've collected, is it better to choose option A or option B? Alternatively (or additionally), you could imagine as vividly as possible what your life might be like (for example, three, six or twelve months from now) if you chose option A and then do the same for option B. This time-projection procedure helps you to look back at the present less daunted by the decision you're going to make.
6. Make your decision without any further debate. Even if it's very close, go for the option which overall has the slight edge. Make a commitment to implement it, and then implement it. Even if you make a wrong decision, you will often be happier in the longer term because at least you made the effort and can learn from your experience which will then inform your next decision. Endless rumination only prolongs the agony of indecision, for example, 'Should it be A or should it be B? I really don't know. What if I choose A, and everything goes wrong? My life will be a mess.'

Creativity

Furnham states that 'Decision making is both a creative and an analytical task' (1996: 36). We've already discussed ways of carefully and critically evaluating alternatives before arriving at a decision. Creativity, on the other hand, involves a process called divergent thinking. This involves taking risks with your thinking in ways that may defy logic, appear absurd and seem foolish to other people. As such, creative thinking frequently involves the temporary suspension of critical thinking to enable new ideas to develop, new associations to form and new perspectives to emerge in your mind. In this section, we look at what blocks you from thinking creatively, developing new ideas and implementing them.

'What will people think of me?'

This is a major obstacle to thinking and acting in unfamiliar ways as you overvalue the opinions others hold of you (for example, 'My friends will think I'm a crank if I tell them I want to try and design a new toothbrush. They're a pretty level-headed bunch so I expect they're right'). You stifle your creativity because you might be frowned upon, laughed at or condemned. Even when wild and spontaneous thinking is actively encouraged such as at brainstorming sessions (that is, letting your imagination rip in order to generate, for example, many ideas for a new advertising jingle), some members of a brainstorming group will still hold back or only present 'safe' ideas because they fear their contribution will be evaluated negatively and they'll be revealed as foolish (Furnham, 1996).

What is the worst thing that will happen to you if people mock you? Feeling very uncomfortable? Or receiving confirmation of your own doubts? We would suggest that you tolerate feeling uncomfortable as you try something new, that you have nothing to learn or value from people who are only interested in putting you down, and that it's natural to have doubts about breaking the bounds of conventional behaviour without letting these doubts inhibit you from doing so. As Hauck says: 'Psychological slaves have chains on their brains, not on their legs. You break them by risking more pain [laughter or ridicule]. The risk is often worth the subsequent gain' (1981b: 70–71).

Creative suppression (Knaus, 1998)

You may believe that you have some creative talent and would like to write a book, compose music or paint a picture. You have made some occasional attempts to get your creative juices flowing but these usually prove fruitless, reinforcing your doubts about your creative abilities (for example, 'Why don't I just admit it: I haven't got any talent'). What holds you back from persisting with your artistic endeavours? Sharon highlighted a common problem which I (MN) discussed with her.

SHARON: I'm waiting for inspiration to come and then it will all flow; the book will suddenly come together. I know that's silly and clichéd, crap really.

MICHAEL: And what do you do with your time while waiting for the inspiration to come?

SHARON: Not much. I waste it on unimportant activities and then get frustrated because I'm not getting on with the book. I feel like giving up sometimes.

MICHAEL: But have you really started yet?

SHARON: What do you mean by that?

MICHAEL: Well, work on your book whether or not you're inspired. How do you know you won't produce some good work even though you start off in an uninspired state?

SHARON: I don't know because I don't try.

MICHAEL: Exactly. So persist with it despite feeling anxious and frustrated that nothing will emerge on that day or in that week.

SHARON: You mean just slog away at it and stop all this nonsense that I can't be creative unless I'm inspired.

MICHAEL: Right. Don't slouch around the house all day wailing 'Muse, where art thou?' Develop a robust outlook: creativity coupled with self-discipline may eventually realise your ambition of having a book published.

SHARON: I know that's right – some of my favourite writers speak of their daily work schedules . . . but they can say that because they're successful, can't they?

MICHAEL: But how did they get to be and stay successful?

SHARON: Okay, I'm still trying to avoid that uninspired slog.

MICHAEL: Do you want to spend the rest of your life torturing yourself as an author manqué, what could have been but never was?

SHARON: I know people like that who always wanted to be actors or painters but wouldn't take the risk of not making it or being exposed as talentless. I don't want to go down that route.

MICHAEL: Then work your socks off to get your book published and that won't come till you've written it and that won't happen until you invest your time and energy in something you really, greatly want – stop dithering, be determined.

SHARON: I think my slogan will be: 'Be determined, not defeatist.'

Creativity is not something that is usually on tap (for example, 'I've got a spare hour so I'll knock out another chapter') but you're likely to have more creative periods if you push yourself to work hard on your project, even though it's frustrating, until another period emerges. By doing this you will avoid what Knaus calls 'the eternal plight' of the frustrated artist: 'Waiting for moments of inspiration while suffering from a lack of accomplishment' (1998: 153).

'I'm not creative'

In the above example, Sharon believed she had some talent but wasn't organising herself or her time in order to try and fulfil that talent. With this block, you genuinely believe that you're not creative, so you convince yourself not to make an ass of yourself trying to be. Like being decisive, you may believe that you're either creative or not creative rather than allowing for some degree of creativity (when people say, for example, they can't paint they usually mean like Rembrandt or Rubens; with these masters in mind, no wonder they daren't pick up a paintbrush and disgrace themselves). The first question to ask is: have you really applied yourself to some activity in order to determine if you have some creative potential such as creating more exotic menus rather than the standard fare you serve up or trying your hand at landscape gardening to transform the view from your kitchen window?

In addition to making a fool of yourself, you may baulk at the discomfort and strangeness involved in stepping outside of your established boundaries and attempting 'to boldly go where you haven't been before'. You will need to tolerate this discomfort and strangeness phase until your artistic side seems more natural to you and could lead eventually to some pleasant surprises, for example, the local paper publishes some of your poetry.

Another block may be your belief that you have to be intelligent to be creative, for example, 'I'm not an arty-farty sort of person. I never went to university, art school or anything like that; in fact, I left school with hardly any qualifications.' As Butler and McManus point out, 'Creativity . . . is only weakly correlated with intelligence. Characteristics such as nonconformity, confidence, curiosity, and persistence are at least as important as intelligence in determining creativity' (2000: 50). Taking the risk of venturing into uncharted territory (for example, 'I fancy having a bash at pottery') will at least give you some idea of your creative potential while continually wondering 'if I have the brains for it' will not.

Creating a 'new' self

Some of the people we see in coaching have sought professional help before for their difficulties or have expended a lot of effort trying to resolve them but without much success. Such individuals often state as their goal for change what clearly hasn't worked previously (for example, 'I want to find a way to make my colleagues respect me'). We ask:

'Why reproduce in coaching a failed strategy?' The usual reply is 'I don't know' or 'What else can I do?' accompanied by a shrug of the shoulders. While it might be tempting for us to suggest possible solutions, it's often counterproductive because this will stifle the person's 'creative efforts to construct new possibilities' (Mooney and Padesky, 2000: 153). Through Socratic questioning, that is, asking a series of questions to promote insight, better problem-solving and decision-making the person's creative efforts can be stimulated:

MICHAEL: Have you found a way after all these years to make people respect you?

SUSAN: No I haven't.

MICHAEL: Do you think you will ultimately stumble across the answer?

SUSAN: Probably not. What else am I supposed to do?

MICHAEL: How, ideally speaking, would you like to see yourself?

SUSAN: *(ponders)* As more confident I suppose.

MICHAEL: Specifically, what would this confidence look like?

SUSAN: Well, it's sort of feeling comfortable in your own skin, exuding professionalism, as if you're in control, you know what you're doing. It's difficult to be more specific than that.

MICHAEL: Are there people you particularly like or admire who act in this way?

SUSAN: There's a woman at work, Janice, who carries herself in the way that I would like to.

MICHAEL: Could you speak to her?

SUSAN: Yeah, I could do that. She's friendly and approachable. Am I supposed to model myself on her?

MICHAEL: Well, if she reveals what her secret is, what could you do then?

SUSAN: Start trying things out, doing things differently and see what happens. Can't hurt, I suppose.

MICHAEL: In order to be Janice Mark Two or a new and improved Susan?

SUSAN: I'd rather be a new and improved Susan.

MICHAEL: So what's the first step in this process of transformation?

SUSAN: *(smiling)* Talk to Janice.

MICHAEL: Can you foresee any difficulties in talking to her about this?

SUSAN: I think I can manage asking her.

Through talking to Janice, Susan said she obtained a valuable piece of advice: 'Why don't you learn to think well of yourself instead of worrying about and wasting too much time on what others think of you. You live too much in other people's heads.' In order to discover what 'thinking well of myself' actually meant, Susan acted in an 'as if' capacity, that is, behaving as if she did think well of herself even if she didn't particularly believe it at that moment. Some examples: expressing opinions that might incur others' disapproval; giving herself rewards for trying out new behaviours; planning more activities which were designed to please her rather than others; learning to say no to what she considered were unreasonable requests; and spending much less time in the company of people who weren't particularly friendly towards her. Acting 'as if' was the creative inspiration for Susan to develop new possibilities for herself and 'give me a view of myself that I didn't think I was capable of seeing, if that makes sense. Also, I believe I was earning the respect of some of my colleagues through comments they made to me. Not bad.' As Kleinke (1991: 89) says:

> 'There is plenty of psychological research to document a fact we all know from our own experience.
> If you want to be,
> Act as if you are,
> And you will become.'

Conclusion

Change involves risk. Risk-taking enables you to develop confidence, self-acceptance in the face of setbacks, learning from mistakes and the chance of achieving important goals. Risk-taking is held back by indecision or made unnecessarily perilous by impulsive decision-making. The potential risks and gains of a particular course of action need to be considered carefully. Decision-making also involves being creative, which invites you to suspend temporarily your critical faculties while you let your imagination soar. Once back on earth, you can evaluate these new ideas in terms of their usefulness in helping you to overcome blocks to change and fostering new ways of thinking and acting.

Chapter 10

Understanding the personal change process

Introduction

Nothing is constant. Change occurs whether you welcome it or fight against it. You cannot be bypassed by change – you're ineluctably caught up in it. You have only to examine your life in the previous six or twelve months to see changes, maybe small and subtle or big and spectacular, some things improving, some things not, and you don't have to be clairvoyant to see that the same process lies ahead of you. The important point is how to make the process of change work beneficially for you (for example, improved well-being) rather than counterproductively (for example, increase in personal distress). For example, Derek was made redundant but quickly made plans to retrain while his friend, Tony, would not accept this reality, wanted his old job back and eventually slipped into depression. In this chapter, we examine what's involved in understanding and negotiating the process of personal change by describing a number of stages to go through.

Stage 1: admit that you have a problem and take responsibility for it

Before admitting to a problem, you have to be aware that you have one. Others may be aware of it by pointing out changes in your mood and behaviour (for example, increasingly preoccupied, keeping friends at a distance), but you deny that anything is wrong. Awareness that something is wrong may gradually dawn when you notice how uncomfortable or out-of-sorts you feel; problems are piling up which you can't avoid any longer or a crisis erupts (for example, your partner threatens to leave if you don't pull yourself together) – all of which forces you to the conclusion that all is not well in your life. Admitting that you have a problem (for example, you're not coping with workplace pressures or your drinking is getting out of control) can become a problem. Shame is one of the biggest blocks to admitting you have a problem because you're revealing to others what you believe is a weakness or inadequacy and you'll probably be rejected, condemned or mocked for it (for example, your friends find out about your sexual impotence and make jokes: 'We were right about him after all – he really is a limp dick!'). As Gilbert observes, 'Of all the emotions that are likely to reduce our ability to be helped, to reach out to others and to treat ourselves with compassion, shame is the most important and destructive' (1997: 174).

In order to avoid experiencing shameful feelings, you may deny you have a problem, try to cover it up or blame it on others (for example, 'You make me lose my temper with all your constant nagging'). A very important aspect of admitting to a problem is accepting yourself for having it, irrespective of how others may judge you (this might seem like a tall order but it's essential if you want to make progress). Admitting to a problem means taking responsibility for your thoughts, feelings and actions without blaming yourself, others, society, fate or fortune for them (for example, 'These angry outbursts are my doing and not your fault even though I blamed you for them in the past'). Taking responsibility means that the days of excuses and rationalisations are over with and you're now focused on regaining control over yourself and your life. As we saw in the chapter on resilience, asking for help is a sign of strength, not weakness, as a truly resilient person uses a variety of resources to get through tough times.

Stage 2: be specific about your problem

You will probably find it hard to solve a problem if you discuss it in vague terms (for example, 'It's something about relationships'). In order to make the problem clear, be as specific as you can about it as demonstrated in this coaching session I (MN) conducted with Alison.

MICHAEL: We need to find out what the 'something' refers to. Does it occur in all relationships or just particular ones?

ALISON: It's really with my husband's friends. I feel uneasy around them.

MICHAEL: Do you know what you're uneasy about in their company?

ALISON: Well, like my husband, they've all been to university and they're intelligent, sophisticated and cultured.

MICHAEL: And if they are . . .?

ALISON: I feel uncultured around them, like I'm a bit of a philistine really. I think that's the problem.

MICHAEL: How would you describe a philistine?
ALISON: Stupid really. They should be interested in arts and culture but they couldn't care less . . . like me.

Stage 3: identify your troublesome emotion

We discussed troublesome emotions such as anxiety, depression, guilt, shame, anger and hurt in Chapter 1. To recap, these are emotions that reoccur in a number of situations in your life, seem excessive when the situations are viewed objectively by you, and remain unresolved. They are neither incapacitating nor do they greatly diminish the quality of your life. When identifying the emotion, avoid vague descriptions of it such as 'I feel bad' or 'I feel as if things are not right'. Which of the above troublesome emotions does 'bad' and 'things are not right' refer to? Pinpointing the emotion is the starting point for identifying the thoughts and beliefs underlying it. As we said elsewhere in this book, CBC is not interested in negative thoughts per se but only those that are directly connected to troublesome emotions and unhelpful behaviours (one client called them 'emotional thoughts'). Alison said she felt 'uneasy' in her husband's friends' company, so I asked her which emotion this referred to:

ALISON: Which emotion? Well, I feel uncomfortable, on edge.
MICHAEL: Uncomfortable, on edge, uneasy could refer to anxiety, anger, hurt, for example, so it's important to pin it down.
ALISON: Oh, I see. It's definitely anxiety. I get butterflies in my stomach hoping I don't say the wrong thing.
MICHAEL: Such as . . .
ALISON: Well, because I'm going to be asked something about the arts and I'll probably make a fool of myself. Saying I like a painter's work but can't think of one painting he did or if I make a stab at it probably mention a painting he didn't do.
MICHAEL: So you're anxious about saying the wrong thing about the arts in front of your husband's friends.
ALISON: That's right.

Stage 4: identify the aspect of the situation that you are most troubled about

Why is this important? Because if you can cope with what you see as the worst aspect of the problem, then the other aspects won't seem so intimidating, scary or overwhelming when you come to deal with them.

For example, your friends take advantage of you with your complicity because you're afraid of being friendless and socially isolated. If you could visualise yourself being alone and drawing strength from your own company, this may encourage you to stand up to your friends and also stop being complicit in your own exploitation. Whether they change their ways or expel you from the group is now less important to you as you can cope with either outcome. In Stage 3, Alison thought that being a philistine around her husband's cultured friends was the real problem but she wasn't sure.

MICHAEL: Shall we see if being a philistine is the aspect of the problem you are most anxious about?

ALISON: Okay.

MICHAEL: If your attitude was 'I couldn't care less about being cultured or what you think of me for being a philistine', would you still be anxious?

ALISON: If I really believed that, then, no, I wouldn't be. I'm anxious about being seen by my husband's friends as uncultured. That's the problem.

MICHAEL: Shall we explore what it means to you to be seen like that?

ALISON: Okay.

MICHAEL: So, what does it mean to you to be seen as uncultured by his friends?

[I'm teasing out the personal meaning in each of Alison's responses in order to follow them to their logical conclusion. I assume that each response is temporarily true in order to arrive at her core meaning or belief. This process is called the downward arrow technique and is discussed in Chapter 1.]

ALISON: *(thinking hard)* Hmm. Well, if they see me as uncultured, stupid then he might too.

MICHAEL: And if he does see you as uncultured, stupid . . .?

ALISON: Then he might look at me differently, as if he is really seeing me for the first time and doesn't like what he sees.

MICHAEL: And if he doesn't like what he sees . . .?

ALISON: Then he'll leave me for someone intelligent and cultured.

MICHAEL: What does that mean about you if he leaves you for someone like that?

ALISON: *(eyes moistening)* That I'm inferior, not good enough. That idea has always been lurking somewhere in my head.

[Alison's core belief has been uncovered.]

MICHAEL: Is that what you're most anxious about: if your husband left you for someone cultured and intelligent, then your long-held belief about your inferiority would really be true, confirmed in your mind?

ALISON: *(slowly nodding)* Yes, unfortunately. The strange thing is most of the time I'm happy and that belief doesn't trouble me, it's just that sometimes when my husband and some of his friends get excited about going to the Glyndebourne Festival [annual festival of opera] for example, I feel left out as I don't feel the same excitement or interest. That's when the belief comes to mind even though I still go with him. I like the picnics and looking at what people are wearing and how they're behaving, not the opera though.

Stage 5: select your goals for change

Goals are the desired outcomes or results that you want for yourself. Though goal-selection may seem relatively easy to do, there are a number of difficulties to watch out for. These include:

- Identifying a goal which is outside of your control such as 'I want my partner to stop taking me for granted'. In this example, you want someone else to change rather than yourself. You have given your partner the power to achieve your goal, and what happens if he's not interested in achieving it for you? To bring the goal back within your control, you need to ask yourself what you can start doing (for example, learning to be assertive) in order to bring to your partner's attention your dissatisfactions with his behaviour. Your new approach may then influence him in making constructive changes in his own behaviour towards you.

- Selecting short-term or quick fix goals which don't address the underlying problems. In the above example, you may decide to put up with his behaviour in order 'to let sleeping dogs lie' and thereby avoid rows and uncomfortable silences in the house. The real unarticulated problem might be your fear that if you antagonise him he will leave you. If you were able to imagine yourself coping resourcefully with living alone (long-term goal) this might then encourage you to persist in trying to reform your present relationship. Also, if you remove the fear of living alone you will not bring this inhibiting and self-defeating attitude into your next relationship.

- Stating your goal in negative terms such as 'I don't want to keep on feeling unconfident'. How do you want to feel then? Getting rid of something means putting something else in its place otherwise you will be changing in a vacuum. So you might say, 'I want to feel more confident', and then start planning and implementing what specific steps in specific situations will lead to the specific outcomes you want which thereby turns a fuzzy goal into a clear one, for example, 'I'm now freely speaking up at meetings, defending my viewpoint whereas before I was reluctant to speak and quickly backed down when someone disagreed with me. I now feel more confident when I go to a meeting.'

- Selecting goals which are unrealistic as they're outside of your capabilities such as 'I must be highly competent at all times'. Such a perfectionistic goal denies your human fallibility and is likely to cause you considerable distress when not realised and confirm in your mind that you're incompetent. A more realistic goal may be to increase your level of competency in specific areas and establish benchmarks to evaluate your progress. Other unrealistic goals may be ones that are set too low in order to avoid experiencing failure. For example, you may select just getting a pass in your exam rather than striving for higher grades: 'Unfortunately, the result is usually as inconsequential as the goal itself and often feels like a "hollow victory" with no sense of accomplishment' (Cormier and Cormier, 1985: 224). If you want to produce a good performance or even a personal best, then select difficult goals rather than easy ones: 'This follows from the fact that people direct their behaviour towards goal achievement, so that difficult goals produce more effective behaviour than easy ones' (Arnold, Cooper and Robertson, 1995: 220–221).

- Feeling calm or unmoved in the face of negative life events. This stoical stance may seem initially desirable but presumably your real intention is to tackle such negative events rather than let the world fall down around your ears. Being stoical may be appropriate while facing the dentist's drill, but not if you're unemployed and need to get a job to pay the mortgage.

- Stating your goals in general instead of specific terms, for example, 'I want to lose two stone in weight' rather than 'I want to feel happier'. The general goal is based on vague yearnings while the specific goal is precise and focused and enables you to shape your behaviour (for example, diet, exercise) to attain it. Also, achieving your target weight is one step closer to feeling happier; adding more specific goals to your list (for example, going on adventure weekends and singles' holidays) may eventually bring you the general goal that several months earlier seemed just a pipe dream. Transforming a general, vague goal into clear, specific ones provides you with an action plan for change.

• Setting goals that may conflict with your ethical standards. For example, you may believe that trust is the basis of a loving and enduring relationship, but you decide to lie to your partner about the money you lost through gambling in order not to upset her. The guilt you feel 'eats away' at you, however, because you're 'living a lie' and the relationship suffers accordingly. In line with your ethical standards, you eventually decide to tell the truth (for example, 'I feel so much better now'), face the consequences (for example, your partner feels let down and keeps her distance from you for several days) and promise to stop gambling.

Goals, once decided upon, are not set in concrete and may have to be altered in the light of information gathered from your goal-directed actions. For example, you may decide to reduce gradually to zero your cigarette intake over a month-long period; but after several days you realise you're just torturing yourself with a slow withdrawal programme and decide to stop there and then and tough it out until the cravings eventually disappear.

I now turn to a discussion of Alison's goals for change.

MICHAEL: You said that the problem was feeling uneasy, anxious around your husband's friends in case you were revealed as uncultured. When we explored the meaning of being uncultured you came to the conclusion that you were inferior and your husband might leave you for someone cultured and intelligent. Okay, so far?

ALISON: Yes, I'm following. So what do I do about it?

MICHAEL: Well, you could ask your husband's friends or your husband if they or he see you as uncultured.

ALISON: I'm sure that they don't – or at least most of them – and he doesn't. It's just my insecurities.

MICHAEL: So if they didn't see you like that, how would you feel in their company?

ALISON: More relaxed.

MICHAEL: What would happen if you met new friends of your husband?

ALISON: *(ponders)* The anxiety would come back for the same reasons. Back to square one.

MICHAEL: So is asking others if they see you as uncultured the solution to your problems?

ALISON: No, that solution won't last. I'm expecting them to solve my problem, to make me feel better about myself.

MICHAEL: So what solution has more chance of lasting and is within your control?

ALISON: Not seeing myself as inferior. I would like to leave that behind.

MICHAEL: In terms of a goal for change, it's better to be working towards something positive rather than simply saying what you don't want or what you want to leave behind.

ALISON: I could learn to be cultured by going to the ballet, opera, art galleries, that sort of thing.

MICHAEL: Is that because you truly want to do that or to gain the approval of others through doing it?

ALISON: *(sighs deeply)* Gain the approval of others. Oh dear – the wrong reasons again.

MICHAEL: So how would you like to see yourself in your own terms?

ALISON: That I can accept myself for following my own interests, being my own person, not trying to play a role I don't believe in, and I certainly don't play the role well.

MICHAEL: If you could believe that, being your own person, how do you think your life would be?

ALISON: Well, I would be genuinely relaxed, I wouldn't make myself anxious around my husband's friends, I'd feel more confident and not give myself such a hard time. Sounds so simple when I say it like that.

MICHAEL: Any drawbacks to being like that?

ALISON: *(musing)* Any drawbacks? I suppose what effect it might have on my marriage.

MICHAEL: Which might be what?

ALISON: Er . . . I'm not sure. My husband has always said that he married me for me, not whether I visit art galleries or go the opera. I don't know really. Just a vague feeling I suppose. My husband has more confidence in me than I have in myself.

MICHAEL: If this vague feeling becomes clearer then we can examine it. So do you want to pursue this goal of accepting yourself on your own terms?

ALISON: I do. It's about time that I did.

Stage 6: challenge and change core beliefs

The three criteria of logic, reality-testing and helpfulness are used to examine core beliefs. We will use the example of failure to demonstrate this examination process.

1. Logic. If you have experienced some failures in your life (for example, loss of a job, end of a relationship), how does it logically follow that you're a failure as a person? You might reply that it does, but would you condemn your children, partner or friends in a similar way for their failures? The usual answer we receive is 'no' which then leads to our next question: 'What makes you so special that you deserve self-condemnation while you're compassionate and understanding towards others?' The issue to decide for yourself is whether your arguments make sense or are unsound, that is, they don't hold up when examined. We would argue that the latter is the case and state that you can never be a failure as a person no matter how many times you fail – you have intrinsic worth as a human being irrespective of your failures in life. We would also argue that labelling yourself as a success is similarly illogical as there are many aspects to being you, not just having a string of successes in your life. Would you still call yourself a success if you were demoted at work?

2. Reality-testing. Does your belief reflect empirical reality? Your subjective viewpoint is compared with your objective experience: if you're a failure as a person, then all you can ever do is fail at every single thing you attempt. Is that an accurate description of your life? Obviously not because you're successful at some things and fail at others. Weighing evidence dispassionately can help you to make more accurate appraisals of your behaviour and life as it actually is. When some people tell me (MN) they're failures, I ask them, for example, how they were able to organise themselves successfully in order to get to the coaching session on time. Reality-testing encourages you to act in the role of a personal scientist by viewing your beliefs and ideas as assumptions instead of as facts. Gathering evidence helps you to confirm, modify or reject these assumptions. Being a personal scientist can be difficult for some clients though, as they may undermine their experiments in order to reach a preferred conclusion, for example, giving up a task after several unsuccessful attempts ('I told you I couldn't do it') rather than patiently persisting with it and carefully evaluating what went wrong with the previous attempts. One client later admitted that on each occasion he angrily rushed through the task hoping to 'ruin it'.

3. Helpfulness. Does the idea that you're a failure help you to overcome your problems and feel better? This is rarely the case though you might argue that calling yourself a failure may motivate you to do better. We see this as a demotivating strategy as you keep on trying to prove what you're not (a failure) rather than working on

how you would like to see yourself such as 'reasonably successful'. Spelling out the short- and long-term consequences of keeping the idea that you're a failure can often be the most powerful argument for surrendering it.

Developing self-acceptance

You're neither inferior nor superior as a person for having or not having problems. So what are you then? As we have argued throughout this book, you're a fallible (imperfect) human being who refuses to rate yourself on the basis of your actions or characteristics but does rate those aspects of yourself which you wish to change or improve (for example, 'I can accept myself for having panic attacks but I really wish I didn't have them; so I will be seeking professional help to overcome them'). Without self-acceptance, you may be continually side-tracked from problem-solving by shame-fuelled self-denigration (for example, 'I'm weak and pathetic for having panic attacks'). We often demonstrate self-acceptance through the use of the 'big I/little i' diagram (Lazarus, 1977; see Figure 10.1).

Hauck calls the self 'every conceivable thing about you that can be rated' (1991b: 33). The big 'I' stands for the self and the little 'i's represent every conceivable thing about you that can be rated (for example, having or not having a job or relationship, hair style, height, age, weight, lying to a friend, giving money to charity) – the list is limitless. The mistake is to assume that some of the little 'i's equal the complexity and totality of the self (for example, 'I lied to my friend, therefore I'm no good'); you could equally say that giving money to charity makes you a good person. Both descriptions of you would be wholly inaccurate. Before we move on, it's important to point out that acceptance of others is as equally important as self-acceptance: rate others' ideas, behaviours, traits but not them as a person, for example, 'I accept you as a fallible human being, but I certainly don't accept your ludicrous idea that women are inferior to men.'

You may think that this idea of self-acceptance is far-fetched (for example, 'Of course you're a failure if you make mistakes'), but we would bet that you don't rate your children on the basis of their behaviour (for example, 'You've been naughty at school. Therefore you're a thoroughly bad little boy who will never change'). So we would urge you not to do it to yourself. In essence, when you concentrate on the big 'I' you are self-focused and likely to be self-attacking, whereas with your attention on the little 'i's you are in a problem-solving and goal-orientated frame of mind (even if the goal is to accept without unduly upsetting yourself what you can't change).

You may have similar rating tendencies towards your role. For example, as a mother or manager, you could construct a big 'M' containing lots of little 'm's and criticise and improve where possible the little 'm's without using them to label the big 'M' (in terms of roles, you could go from A [for example, actor] to Z [for example, zookeeper]).

If you disagree with the concept of self-acceptance or see it as unattainable, then strive to develop a multidimensional identity: 'People who have a one-dimensional view of themselves are very limited. They don't have a broad foundation of personal resources to fall back on when facing difficult challenges' (Kleinke, 1991: 208). For example, if your work is your worth, what will happen to your self-esteem when you lose your job or retire? If your partner is your reason for living, your thoughts might turn to self-harm if he leaves you or dies? Therefore, 'good copers have a life philosophy of developing their personal identity along many dimensions' (Kleinke, 1991: 208). In other words, don't put all your eggs in one or two baskets.

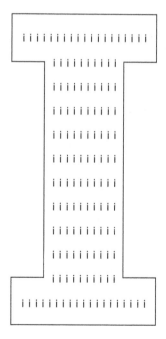

Figure 10.1 The big I/little i diagram.

Alison's belief of inferiority is examined using logic, reality-testing and helpfulness:

MICHAEL: In terms of logic, how does it make sense to say that you're inferior as a person because you see yourself as uncultured?

ALISON: I suppose it doesn't make sense but I don't know why.

MICHAEL: Would you call people who are short or blind or live in council houses or left school without any qualifications inferior people?

ALISON: Of course I wouldn't.

MICHAEL: Why not?

ALISON: Because they can't help being short, blind or living in council houses. Those things about them don't make them inferior.

MICHAEL: What would make them inferior in your eyes?

ALISON: Well . . . er . . . nothing I can think of. They're just people coping with the circumstances of their lives. I don't know what else to say.

MICHAEL: If nothing you can think of would make other people inferior, how does being uncultured make you inferior?

ALISON: I don't know but I would usually say that it does. Okay, I don't know but I need to think about it more.

MICHAEL: Okay, let's ask if your belief is realistic: if you were inferior, what evidence would you need to prove it?

ALISON: I suppose other people would treat me as if I were inferior. Some people have been rude to me sometimes.

MICHAEL: Is that evidence of your inferiority or their impoliteness?

ALISON: Their impoliteness.

MICHAEL: Let's focus on this issue of inferiority: if the world or other people truly saw you as inferior, how would you be treated?

ALISON: I suppose I'd be rejected, despised, always pushed to the back of the queue, pointed at and ridiculed, a permanent second-class citizen.

MICHAEL: Is that your actual experience?

ALISON: Of course not, but I sometimes wonder if some people see me as inferior for not having a university degree.

MICHAEL: If some people do see you that way, where's the proof that it makes you inferior?

ALISON: The proof is in here (touching her head) not out there (pointing towards the window). I just believe sometimes that I should be reading Shakespeare instead of the *Sun*, and watching ballet rather than the soaps. That's all.

MICHAEL: Even if your cultural preferences are not what you would like them to be or are lacking in balance, this might be an occasion for regret but, again, where is the evidence that you, Alison, are inferior if you don't read Shakespeare or superior if you do?

ALISON: I suppose my bearings are all confused. I've never really thought about the things you're asking me.

MICHAEL: Well, the time has now arrived! Let's look at the issue of help-fulness. Where does it get you believing you're inferior?

ALISON: Nowhere. I'm just worried sometimes that I might be exposed as an ignoramus when asked my views on a new play that I've seen or something like that. I can't think of any good that it does me.

MICHAEL: If that's the case, why do you stick with a belief that does you no favours?

ALISON: *(long pause)* Well, I suppose seeing myself as inferior niggles away at me to improve my mind and eventually have a higher opin-ion of myself.

MICHAEL: And how far away are you from that higher opinion of yourself?

ALISON: About a million miles.

MICHAEL: Okay. We've had an introductory look at your belief that you're inferior to see if it's logical, realistic and helpful. What happened?

ALISON: My belief failed all three tests but I'm not convinced yet. So what's next then?

MICHAEL: Going over these and other arguments again and again until you are able to see that calling yourself inferior is illogical, unreal-istic and unhelpful. At the same time, we need to look at develop-ing an alternative self-image based on what you wanted which was, quote, 'being my own person', unquote.

ALISON: Now I'll have to find out what that really means.

I explained the 'big I/little i' diagram to Alison by circling some of the little 'i's representing aspects of herself (for example, being uncultured, not going to university, her anxiety) and then judging herself, her totality as a human being – the big 'I' – on the basis of these little 'i's. I asked her about her good points and I circled some more little 'i's (for example, keeping fit, being a good cook, doing charity work) and asked her if these good points totally described her complexity as a human being any more accurately than her bad points did? She began to see that it was illogical to judge herself on the basis of particular actions, characteristics or expe-riences and that striving to accept herself as a fallible human being could eventually overcome her self-rating as inferior and prevent or minimise any further self-rating. Also, as human beings are in a state of flux, little 'i's will disappear from the big 'I' (for example, giving up smoking, losing your hair) while new ones (for example, reaching forty years of age, changing careers) will be added. Again, how can your continual life changes be summed up by a single label?

Alison was worried, however, that self-acceptance implied complacency and stasis ('I might not bother with anything or push myself if I learn self-acceptance'). I (MN) replied that self-acceptance is the basis for personal development and goal-directed behaviour, and that by giving up unhealthy absorption in self-denigration she would be able to reclaim valuable time and energy to invest in new projects. If she worked hard to internalise self-acceptance, then in three, six or twelve months' time she could assess the benefits of this new way of viewing herself.

Stage 7: strengthen your new outlook

In strengthening your new beliefs, it's important to think and act in ways that are consistent with them and stop or reduce thinking and acting in ways that are inconsistent with them. In other words, ensure that your new beliefs, thoughts and behaviours are working together. For example, if your new outlook is to be open and honest about your gay lifestyle, then your thoughts (for example, 'No more lies or self-deception. Now it's time to face people and let them see the real me') and behaviours (for example, taking your partner to meet your parents and friends) need to reflect it. Thoughts (for example, 'Maybe I haven't tried hard enough to be heterosexual') and behaviours (for example, not being seen in public with your partner) which militate against internalising your new outlook need to be challenged in order to weaken their hold on you.

Continual practice in adopting new ways of thinking and behaving may produce a puzzling phenomenon – you don't feel any different (for example, 'I don't call myself a loser any more, I tackle problems as soon as they appear instead of procrastinating over them, but I still feel rather low. How come?'). The reason for this is because emotional change often lingers behind changes in your thoughts and behaviours and therefore takes time to 'catch up'. Significant emotional change usually occurs when you have deep conviction in your new outlook; so don't become discouraged when your feelings appear not to budge in the early stages of the change process.

You will not believe in your new ideas until you put them into daily practice in forceful and persistent ways (for example, staying in situations you previously avoided in order to overcome your panic symptoms). Acting on them occasionally or in a milk-and-water manner will not usually produce much, if any, real change (for example, 'I've tried to stay in those situations but I feel so uncomfortable and jittery that I have to leave'). Internalising a new outlook involves a commitment from you 'to doing the work necessary to bring about the changes you want. Without this commitment, your efforts may very well be sporadic and half-hearted, and your gains will be slow, accidental, and incomplete' (Grieger, 1991: 39). So reflect on what genuine commitment really means and to nudge your thinking along, remember the crucial distinction between action tendencies (what you may or may not do in any given situation) and completed actions (what you actually did in that situation). Genuine commitment would mean a high percentage of completed actions in pursuit of your goals while a high percentage of action tendencies – you failed to follow through – shows you have a lukewarm relationship to commitment.

Your commitment to change and the hard work associated with it may be undermined by five major traps.

Trap 1. 'I cannot take constructive action until I am comfortable'

If you believe that only when you feel comfortable will you be able to initiate change, then change will be delayed indefinitely. When you start taking constructive action you will feel uncomfortable at first but as Ellis points out: 'Make yourself do the work you dislike, force yourself to do it and do it. Deliberately push yourself to be uncomfortable – yes, uncomfortable – until you finally find the work easy and comfortable.' (2002: 155). By courting discomfort now you will be able to make yourself reasonably comfortable later.

Trap 2. 'I cannot take constructive action because I do not have a sense of control'

A sense of control is gradually established by venturing forth and accepting that you currently feel out of control – accepting that you're out of control is, paradoxically, the starting point in developing control. For example, overcoming your panic attacks will only come by your determination to stay in those fearful situations until your symptoms subside. Through daily practice of this 'staying-in-there' technique, you gain control over your panic. If you keep on telling yourself that 'I must be in control' *before* undertaking action, you will only reinforce the idea that you're out of control and remain stuck with your panic symptoms.

Trap 3. 'I cannot act differently because I do not feel competent yet'

Competence is not usually achieved in one fell swoop. Trial and error is usually the order of the day. As one client said, tongue in cheek, 'I want to avoid all trial and make no errors!' So expect to act incompetently, but through learning from your mistakes you will notice a transition from acting incompetently to performing competently. It's highly doubtful that you will be able to bypass this learning process.

Trap 4. 'I cannot take new action which is strange to me because I do not feel confident to do so'

It's perfectly natural to feel unconfident about acting in new and strange ways – how could it be otherwise? Unless you persist in these 'strange' actions and accept that this is the way it should (realistically) be if you want to become confident, you will probably give up and return to familiar ways that you actually want to change. The more you practise these new actions the quicker they will feel less strange and more natural to you. Remember our watchword: 'If you ain't feeling strange, then you ain't experiencing change.'

Trap 5. 'I cannot undertake constructive actions, particularly those which are risky for me, because I do not have the courage to do so'

People who perform courageous acts don't usually say things like 'I felt deeply courageous and that's why I rescued the child from the burning building'. The more usual reply is that they believed it was the right or necessary action at the time even though they were afraid. Gaining courage in facing your fears comes from action, not waiting around until you feel courageous – the longer you wait for the feeling to arrive the more likely you are to convince yourself that 'I haven't got the guts to take these chances' and settle for second-best and a pattern of avoidance.

   With all five traps, there is a paradox at work in personal change: if you want to feel comfortable, be in control, act competently, confidently and courageously, then you first need to feel uncomfortable or out of control, and to act incompetently, unconfidently and uncourageously. So when considering what changes you wish to make in your life, remember that struggle and strangeness come first, success later.

Alison's goal was to 'be my own person'. She continually challenged her belief that she was inferior by using the three criteria of logic, reality-testing and usefulness. To put into practice the idea of self-acceptance, Alison began to tell her husband's friends that she wasn't interested in 'cultural pursuits' and that she much preferred watching *EastEnders* or *Coronation Street* and would explain current plotlines to them (previously she would pretend to hang on to every word they said and try to play the culture vulture). In addition, she would let them see her reading the *Sun* when they arrived at the house and chat to them about the 'shocking' revelations of a pop star's sex life (before, she would hide the newspaper). Even though Alison felt very unconfident and uncomfortable in acting this way, she could see the rationale for it:

ALISON: If I don't put it into practice what we've been discussing, then all this self-acceptance stuff is just pie in the sky.

MICHAEL: Exactly. So how are you getting on?

ALISON: Well, sometimes I overdo my real interest in the *Sun* or *EastEnders* in order to get the point across that they can take or leave me but, whatever their reaction is, the important point is for me not to put myself down.

MICHAEL: What has been their response?

ALISON: Apart from a few comments that the *Sun* can seriously damage your mental health, nothing much really. Some people have asked me why I've suddenly started behaving differently.

MICHAEL: What did you reply?

ALISON: I was honest with them about my previous feelings of inferiority and that I'm learning self-acceptance and no longer trying to pretend what I'm not. I can't believe at times that I'm being so open about these things but it's becoming liberating because I'm worrying less what others think about me.

MICHAEL: What's been the general reaction of your husband's friends?

ALISON: Most of them couldn't really care less. What I thought would happen – like them looking down their noses at me, treating me with contempt – didn't happen, so I was really surprised about that. One or two of them though have been rather snotty about it but I've always thought that they thought my husband married beneath him. Of course, I used to agree with that.

MICHAEL: And now?

ALISON: I don't believe that now but there are days when I start to wobble again and think: 'What does he see in a thicko like me?' But that's to be expected, isn't it?

MICHAEL: Yes it is. Change doesn't remove all your doubts, they just inhibit you less.

ALISON: I can see that. Do you know what? Now that I'm thinking about what I really want for myself instead of trying to get the approval of others, I'm actually considering doing a degree through the Open University because now I'm genuinely interested in it. Bizarre, isn't it?

MICHAEL: Good for you.

Stage 8: generalise your gains to other relevant situations

The gains you make in one situation (for example, tolerating the intense discomfort of repeatedly asking your next-door neighbour to turn down his loud music) can be extended to other difficult interpersonal contexts such as standing your ground with colleagues who try to dump some of their work on you or saying no to friends who may regard you as a taxi service. Don't assume that these gains will automatically transfer to new situations (there will be a snowball effect); in fact, you might have to start from scratch in tackling a different situation (for example, 'I now can give as good as I get with my neighbour, so why do I still walk on eggshells with some of my work colleagues?'). Tolerating discomfort in one context may pose different challenges in another (for example, 'At least with my neighbour I don't have to live with him but with some of my colleagues there will be a bad atmosphere in the office every day which I'll have to put up with. I don't fancy that'). Generally speaking, if you want your gains to extend to other situations, then undertake an action plan to bring this about.

Accepting herself in the face of her husband's friends' presumed or actual disapproval was Alison's first step. She then stopped putting herself in an intellectually subordinate position with those work colleagues who had university degrees (for example, 'I always thought "I'm not as smart as you because I haven't been to university"') and started giving her opinions and arguing her corner (this didn't mean she had to win every argument or attempt to get people to respect her but to signal to herself and others that she no longer saw herself as inferior). Her greatest apprehension was how her husband would react to her new stance 'even though he has told me time and time again that he accepts me for myself'. Instead of going with her husband to cultural events 'which often bored the living daylights out of me', she began pursuing more of her own interests and therefore spent less time in his company. I asked her how he was reacting to this:

ALISON: He's not bothered. He says it's about time I developed my own interests and thought things through for myself. He's been very supportive.

MICHAEL: Okay, let me jump to the worst outcome. How would you react if your husband didn't approve of your new behaviour or only had accepted you as long as you played the obedient wife and not tried to rise above your intellectual station in life?

ALISON: Before I would have been devastated that he only married me because I was an obedient thicko, but now . . . *(long pause)* but now, and if that really was the case, I would try to build a different kind of relationship with him or if that fell apart or he didn't agree with it, then I would end up leaving him – as very sad as that would be. You know, saying these things to you would have been inconceivable just six months ago. I feel for the first time in my life that I'm truly becoming my own person.

Stage 9: maintain your gains

Whether you have made progress and achieved your goals through coaching sessions or a self-initiated change programme, it's important to remember that your gains are unlikely to be maintained unless you consistently work to support them (for example, getting fit is not the same as staying fit – both require sustained effort from you). Even if you work hard to avoid a reactivation of your problems, there is no guarantee that they will disappear for good.

Therefore, in order to minimise the chances of their reappearance, you can list vulnerability factors in your life that might trigger a lapse (stumble) or a relapse (collapse). For example, you might see holiday periods when you're likely to be alone as vulnerable times that could lead back to overeating, inactivity and low mood ('When I spend too much time on my own, the old idea that I'm unlikeable tends to sneak back'). For such occasions, you can prepare an action plan that would involve daily activities, people you could phone or group activities such as adventure weekends – anything that would reduce the time spent alone. Eventually, spending time alone rather than avoiding it would need to be faced as part of your coping and self-acceptance strategy: you choose to spend time with yourself rather than seeing yourself being forced into it because 'no one likes me'.

If you do have a lapse, try to avoid condemning yourself for it (for example, 'I'm weak. I'll never change'). Instead, analyse the factors leading up to it as part of a continuing learning process (for example,

'I deliberately engineered a row with my wife so I could storm out of the house, go to the nearest pub and start drinking again. I used it as an excuse because I still haven't convinced myself yet that alcohol does more harm than good in my life, but I'm getting there'). In this way you can strive to prevent a lapse turning into a relapse. Even if you have a relapse, you can analyse it in the same way to extract learning from it (for example, 'This bender only lasted a couple of days. The last time I went off the rails I was drunk for a week. That's progress').

Maintaining your gains from coaching or your own change programme involves a lifelong commitment to hard work. This initially sounds like a dispiriting message but, from our own experience, we know that the hard work gets easier the more of it you do. So less work now means more effort later while more work now means less effort later.

Alison had been working hard to make self-acceptance a daily reality but sometimes found it hard going:

ALISON: Why didn't I know about all this stuff twenty years ago? I should have known. I feel I've wasted so much time in my life dragging this inferiority complex around with me. I wonder if I'm any happier with this new knowledge.

MICHAEL: Okay, let's start with why you didn't know about this stuff twenty years ago. What's the answer to that?

ALISON: I didn't know about self-acceptance, it was never in my thinking, no one ever explained it to me. It's as simple as that. It's like a secret that's been hidden from me until now.

MICHAEL: So why give yourself a hard time by saying that you should have known what you couldn't possibly have known at the time?

ALISON: I know it's silly but these ideas do cling on.

MICHAEL: If you continue to believe them, argue with them, give them a prominent place in your mind instead of getting bored with them and showing them the door so to speak, then they will cling on.

ALISON: Okay, that makes a lot of sense.

MICHAEL: Now, has all the past twenty years been a waste?

ALISON: It feels like it sometimes, but when I'm thinking clearly I know that's not the case. It's been good and bad, up and down. I suppose like most other people's lives.

MICHAEL: If you spend the next twenty years lamenting the waste of the last twenty, then what?

ALISON: *(laughs)* Forty years of waste!

MICHAEL: Did you think that applying this new knowledge would be straightforward rather than an emotional rollercoaster at times?

ALISON: I suppose I did think it would be easier than it is. I keep on questioning things more now than I ever did before in my life.

MICHAEL: That's part of the change process. Things will start to level out when you feel more at home with your new way of seeing yourself. Are these changes worth persisting with though?

ALISON: Yes. I'm not going to turn back now. I know and hope deep down that what lies ahead of me will be more interesting and exciting than what went before.

MICHAEL: Amen to that!

Conclusion

Between desiring change and achieving it, there are a number of stages to pass through. These stages provide structure to the change process and markers for assessing progress (for example, not taking responsibility for your problem is likely to keep you stranded in Stage 1). Coping successfully with the change process requires you to learn from and adapt to its vicissitudes. Such an outlook will stand you in good stead for present and future problem-solving.

Chapter 11

Putting it all together

Introduction

In the previous chapters, we hope that we've shown you ways of tackling successfully a range of difficulties that will help you to achieve greater personal effectiveness in your life. Definitions of personal effectiveness are, of course, highly subjective, for example, one person may see being assertive in certain situations as her desired outcome while another wants to start his own business. Obviously you will need to establish progress markers to demonstrate that you're moving closer to your goals, for example, starting tasks earlier rather than later, asking for feedback on your performance instead of putting it off, listening to criticism without immediately defending yourself, and removing time-wasting activities from your daily work schedule.

Your view of personal effectiveness will probably change over time as you develop greater competence and confidence in managing difficulties and responding to challenges, for example, risk-taking is now seen by you as an indispensable and exciting part of personal growth whereas before you viewed it apprehensively as containing more dangers than benefits. In this chapter, we focus on what we consider to be the key determinants of increased personal effectiveness.

Self-acceptance

We have discussed this concept repeatedly in this book because we believe it's of central importance in promoting psychological stability. Self-acceptance means that you stop putting yourself down and move your focus to your actions, traits and experiences (for example, 'I made a mess of this situation which I'm going to put right if I can, but I refuse to damn myself because of the mistakes I made'). Self-acceptance greatly reduces the duration, frequency and intensity of your troublesome emotions because you stop attacking yourself which is often at the heart of these emotions. We distinguish self-acceptance from self-esteem: self-acceptance is unconditional – no strings attached – whereas self-esteem is conditional. If you place your worth on a series of hooks (for example, looks, body, friends, job, respect of colleagues, income) and a hook breaks off the wall (for example, you put on a lot of weight during a prolonged illness), you're likely to activate your negative core beliefs from their dormant state and they'll give you hell (for example, 'You're repulsive. How could you have done this to yourself? There's absolutely no excuse for getting hideously fat just because you were ill. No one's going to look at you now').

Sometimes it seems that many psychological problems can be traced to a single source: low self-esteem. The seemingly obvious remedy to these problems is to have high self-esteem, so flood your mind with positive affirmations (for example, 'I'm a good and capable person. If I really believe hard enough in myself good things will come to me') and then your mood and self-image will start to improve. Unfortunately, research shows that, for example, high self-esteem is the result of working hard to get good grades in school, not the cause of good grade achievement (Baumeister and Tierney, 2012). So you're looking in the wrong direction, so to speak, to find higher self-esteem when you need to do the work first before it appears: 'Healthy self-regard comes from finding strengths, working on them and building a skills base. It involves dedication and resolve. And from that investment flows self-esteem' (Furnham, 2012). We believe that having a bedrock of self-acceptance to support your goal-seeking means you're focused on accomplishment rather than using accomplishment to boost your somewhat fragile self-esteem; and with self-esteem, what goes up inevitably comes down as if you're a stock market with your ego rising and falling depending on how your self-estimation is faring this week.

Having said all that, we acknowledge that unconditional self-acceptance is unrealisable because we're imperfect human beings who will on occasions rate our actions and then rate ourselves on the basis of these actions (for example, 'I don't really understand what self-acceptance is, so I must be stupid'). Realistically, strive for much greater self-acceptance thereby keeping to a minimum the times you rate yourself. Self-acceptance helps you to be authentic with yourself by honestly acknowledging your true feelings, beliefs and values rather than trying to convince yourself that you should be other than you are (though this view in no way prevents you from addressing those aspects of yourself you wish to change). Being authentic with others is equally important: you stop trying to seek their approval, 'put on faces' or hide your weaknesses from them (we're not suggesting you make a full and immediate confession of your failings every time you meet someone new – only selective self-exposure when you deem appropriate).

High frustration tolerance (HFT)

We believe that one of the major blocks to change is low frustration tolerance, that is, you want to achieve your longer-term goals but 'throw in the towel' when you encounter setbacks, frustrations, discomfort; in other words, you're not prepared to endure struggle and discomfort. For example, if you want to get out of debt, it will be necessary to forgo or greatly reduce present pleasures (that is, keep a tight rein on your financial outgoings) until the debt is paid off. You may see the perfect sense in this but don't like the idea of austerity living and continue with your pleasures thereby sabotaging your longer-term goal: you stay in debt or even increase it.

The cognitive core of HFT is 'I will tolerate the discomfort in order to reach my goals' – persistence with purpose and another demonstration of your self-control. We don't ask our clients if they feel comfortable about carrying out their goal-related tasks as this seems a counterproductive question. You won't develop HFT if the focus is on feeling comfortable. Much more productive is to discuss with clients the benefits of adopting HFT in order to cope with the difficulties of change. If someone tells you that overcoming personal difficulties can be effortless and they have the solution, instead of whooping with joy, be very sceptical.

Think for yourself

You may think that some of your beliefs are the result of brainwashing (for example, 'Society makes you feel that you're inferior or no good if you're overweight') or given to you by others (for example, 'My partner says I'm a failure, so he must be right'). In both examples, you're accepting *uncritically* these messages instead of directing yourself to 'take a step back and really think about what they're saying'. We would argue that if you do believe you're inferior for being overweight or see yourself as a failure that is because *you* have ultimately chosen to believe these things – they haven't been 'forced' into your head. For example, if the fashion industry started a campaign which said that being overweight was sexy, cool and glamorous, would you automatically agree with this viewpoint and, if you were slim, would you deliberately put on weight?

Another obstacle to clear thinking is over-generalising about yourself, others and the world (for example, 'I'm weak', 'Everyone is against me' and 'Nothing ever goes right'). Instead, view these things along a continuum (that is, seeing events in relative rather than absolute terms) which will help you to develop a more accurate and realistic appraisal of them (for example, 'I have weaknesses and strengths', 'My family and a few friends still support me' and 'Some things go right and some things go wrong'). Try to remain open-minded to alternative viewpoints, assess the reliability and strength of the evidence used by others to support their arguments, take nothing for granted (or, at least, not accept too much on the say-so of others), don't be intimidated by the views of others (for example, experts, gurus, politicians) or prevailing orthodoxies (for example, political correctness) or agree with what you really don't believe because you seek others' approval and don't want to be the odd one out in a group (the famous experiments carried out by Solomon Asch in the 1950s looked at the difficulties of disagreeing with majority opinion). Thinking clearly and honestly can help you to be more independent of thought.

Do remember, however, that being independently minded means that sometimes you will agree with majority opinion because it's right, based on the evidence. To always be against majority opinion shows a contrarian disposition based on the fear of being seen as a conformist which paradoxically undermines your status as an independent thinker – you conform to being a nonconformist!

Be resilient

If your life is struck by misfortune don't give in to despair and helplessness (though these feelings might be difficult to dislodge at times) but commit yourself to finding a way forward that is suited to your own strengths, abilities, temperament and pace. Putting together this bespoke programme will probably take some time and that's why we prefer to talk of coming back from adversity rather than the popular image of bouncing back which can suggest a rapid and near-effortless return to the status quo, but with the possible problem of self-depreciation (for example, 'What's wrong with me?') if you can't find the bounce to put into your recovery.

Resilience is a capacity open to all to learn, not bestowed upon a favoured few. The best way to make yourself more resilient is to choose to face the situations you've been avoiding such as public speaking or standing up to bullies: 'By undertaking acts of voluntary discomfort

. . . we harden ourselves against misfortunes that might befall us in the future' (Irvine, 2009: 112). The adversities we choose to face now help us to prepare for the unchosen and greater adversities that lie ahead.

Take calculated risks

We emphasise calculated risks, not impulsive or foolish ones. Calculated risks are based on considering the short- and long-term consequences of a particular course of action (for example, leaving a relationship, becoming self-employed). Risk-taking can create new and exciting possibilities for you (for example, 'What would I really like to do with my life?') but also, of course, involves failures and setbacks. You may invest a great deal of time and effort in a particular activity which turns out unfavourably; instead of feeling despair, you could shift your viewpoint and remember, as we pointed out in the chapter on resilience, no experience has to be wasted – learning can be extracted from it (others might be helpful in pointing out to you what this learning is if you struggle to see it for yourself). We would suggest that trying and sometimes failing is better than never trying at all.

Learn to accept uncertainty

We live in a world of probability and chance where no absolute guarantees exist (even death might one day be abolished by medical advances). If you demand certainty of success before you embark on various activities, you will probably make yourself paralysed with indecision. Even if someone you completely trusted guaranteed that you would succeed, would you completely believe her? Probably not, because she might be wrong; so even if you get the guarantees you're demanding, your uncertainty doesn't disappear. If you accept uncertainty in life (without having to like it), then you realise

> that judgements and decisions can be made with no guarantee that things will work as planned. Mature, effective people make their decisions based on incomplete knowledge, and responsibly cope with the outcomes of their decisions and learn from each one so as to increase their knowledge for future decisions (Dryden and Matweychuk, 2000: 86).

Instead of endlessly worrying about uncertainties in life, become probabilistic-minded, that is, you think that you'll probably get more of what you want from life and less of what you don't want if you work hard, take risks and are determined.

Self-responsibility

This means that you're ultimately responsible for the way you think, feel and behave no matter what contributed to your present difficulties. For example, you blame your partner's unfaithfulness for making you feel depressed as you believe his behaviour proves you're unattractive. The division of responsibility is actually this: he's responsible for his unfaithfulness and you're responsible for your self-evaluation as unattractive and the resulting depression (for example, 'If I'm unattractive, he will leave me. What can I do to make him desire me again and stop him from going? Why am I so pathetic about all this? Will I ever stop being a doormat?'). Refusing to take responsibility for yourself means you're likely to see yourself as a permanent victim of circumstances instead of someone taking charge of her thoughts, feelings and behaviours and consequently her life. The late and distinguished philosopher, Isaiah Berlin, described self-responsibility in this way:

> I wish my life and decisions to depend on myself, not on external forces of whatever kind. I wish to be the instrument of my own, not of other men's, acts of will. I wish to be a subject, not an object; to be moved by reasons, by conscious purposes, which are my own, not by causes which affect me, as it were, from outside. I wish to be somebody, not nobody; a doer – deciding, not being decided for, self-directed and not acted upon by external nature or by other men as if I were a thing, or an animal, or a slave incapable of playing a human role, that is, of conceiving goals and policies of my own and realising them.
>
> (1998: 203)

While this might be the expressed ideal, in reality, we're all constrained by external forces. Internal forces which constrain us are our self-defeating ideas and beliefs which, as in the above example, promote intrapersonal (internal) conflict and emotional upset, and block goal-attainment. Internal constraints are within our power to identify, challenge and change in order to become more self-directed. By dismantling these internal blocks through the methods we have described in this book, you can experience a greater or new-found sense of personal freedom: 'I'm no longer depressed. I kicked him out for screwing around and gave up this stupid idea that my attractiveness depended on his faithfulness. My attractiveness depends on whether I believe in me, which I now do. The doormat is back where it belongs – outside the front door'). You make the choices for the kind of life you want to lead.

Enlightened self-interest

This is not to be confused with selfishness where you think only about yourself and disregard the interests and desires of others. Enlightened self-interest means putting your own interests first a lot of the time and others' interests, particularly significant others', a close second. The reason that this form of self-interest is enlightened is because if you don't look after yourself, you will not be of much use to yourself or others. For example, if you work consistently long hours you may jeopardise your physical and psychological health, see a decline in your workplace performance and a deterioration in your relationships with your partner, children and friends, and develop a sour disposition. It's important to decide what your priorities are in life (for example, attain physical fitness, gain more qualifications, have more family outings) and then determine whether your time is actually directed towards achieving these important goals.

Enlightened self-interest also needs to be distinguished from selflessness where you disregard your own interests and concentrate on the concerns of others. Selflessness may be pursued for unhealthy reasons. For example, you believe you're not worthy enough to ever put your own interests first (for example, 'I'm no good. Only others count'); therefore, your conclusion that your life should be dedicated to the service of others stems from self-denigratory thinking. If you did believe you had intrinsic worth, however, no more or no less than others, would you still be as willing to devote your life solely to the service of others?

Enlightened self-interest can mean putting others' interests or needs (for example, your children's, your infirm parents') before your own because you choose to for rational reasons (for example, 'I do want to look after my parents as much as I can, but if the time comes when I can no longer cope, then I will consider a residential home for them'). Whether you put your own or others' interests first some or most of the time, the essence of enlightened self-interest is flexibility: you're responding to the requirements of changing circumstances.

Develop vitally absorbing interests

A lot of your time may be taken up with mundane activities that obviously do not excite or absorb you. Therefore, select activities that will fire your imagination and give you a great deal of personal fulfilment (for example, playing golf, writing poetry, going to the opera) but without becoming obsessed about them, as this may throw your life out of kilter (for example, your partner has become a 'golf widow' and is threatening to leave you as 'I never see you any more'). Whatever interests you choose, try not to be deflected from pursuing them by the possible jeers or mockery of others (for example, 'Brass rubbing! I always knew you were a pervert'). A passion for something (as long as it doesn't harm yourself or others) forcefully reminds you of the difference between really living and merely existing.

We sometimes see clients who are disillusioned with ever finding happiness. Each new activity undertaken is interrogated: 'Will *this* make me happy?' These clients make the mistake of putting the search for happiness at the centre of their life. Why this is a mistake has been echoed down the centuries and is here stated by Grayling (2002: 71): 'It has wisely been said that the search for happiness is one of the main sources of unhappiness in the world.' If the search for happiness ends in unhappiness, then how are we to be happy? The solution to this problem also has been stated many times over the centuries and is here summed up by T. E. Lawrence (Lawrence of Arabia): 'Happiness is a by-product of absorption.' If you develop absorbing interests, then happiness will approach you indirectly, sneak up on you, as we might say, when you're not looking. One caveat: don't demand that happiness should now arrive because you've stopped searching for it!

Think and act flexibly

Changing circumstances require adaptive responses from us. For example, we are reliably informed that there are no more jobs for life and, therefore, we will have a number of jobs and careers before we retire (even retirement is now seen as full of opportunities and challenges rather than as a sedate, 'winding down' phase of our life). Whatever the circumstances in your life at any given moment, demanding that they should not exist (for example, 'My partner shouldn't have run off with someone else – what am I to do?'; 'I shouldn't be stuck in this traffic jam when I've got an important meeting to get to') will not make them easier to adjust to or deal with. In all probability, your emotional upsets will intensify as you refuse to accept the grim or frustrating reality of events (for example, depression and withdrawal from social activity; increase in anger).

Research shows that people with good coping skills have learnt to think and act flexibly in the face of adverse events. When the going gets tough there are usually two kinds of thinking open to us: adaptive, tough-minded, problem-solving thinking (for example, 'The shit has hit the fan.

I'll clean the fan') and unadaptive, crumble-minded, making-the-going-even-tougher thinking (for example, 'Why did it hit my fan? Who did this? I don't want to deal with it. Someone make it go away').

Thinking and acting flexibly is also necessary sometimes with enjoyable events such as winning a million pounds on the premium bonds. You might believe that to make up for the hard times in your life you're now going to live an extravagant lifestyle, but within a couple of years your money is gone and you have to fall back on benefits or a low-income job (the hard times have returned). A flexible response to winning the premium bonds would be to enjoy yourself now and invest for the future to provide you with a lifelong income; in other words, the exercise of self-control.

Develop realistic expectations

It's highly unlikely we're going to get everything we want in life or avoid everything that might be painful for us. In addition, much valuable time and energy is wasted on striving for the unattainable. For example, you might believe that the solution to your problems is to be perfect. How many years have you been trying to be perfect and how many more years will it take before you accept that it's beyond your reach? The human condition is an imperfect one. You may initially agree and then say 'but' . . . which means you don't really agree and will still pursue the holy grail of human perfection. Even if you do some things perfectly (task-perfection), this does not and cannot make *you* perfect (self-perfection). Task-perfection cannot be repeated endlessly, for example, a gymnast may get a perfect ten in the floor exercises but doing the same exercises later she stumbles and receives a 9.5.

Alternatively, you could see yourself as highly efficient but fallible – acknowledge your imperfections and accept you will never be free of all of them, and then focus your energies on striving to reach important but realistic goals. So don't waste time on what is truly out of reach.

Learn tolerance

Tolerance means you're willing to allow the existence of other opinions and behaviours (which you might be passionately opposed to) but without having to accept or like them; if you find someone's opinion or behaviour objectionable, then argue against it but without condemning the person for it. Tolerance allows you and others the right to be wrong and thereby reduces the potential for angry confrontations. Hauck states that when you're angry with others for the opinions they hold, you're acting like a dictator: 'Your anger signifies that you don't like another person's actions and therefore his thoughts, and intend to control both from now on against that person's will' (1980: 70). Remember that you can't control what others think or how they behave but you can attempt to change some of their views and actions through reasoned debate. Grayling (2009) suggests that we tend to pride ourselves on being tolerant when we're not really bothered by someone's beliefs or behaviours; when we're bothered, then the hard work of tolerance begins.

Teach others

A key way of deepening your conviction in your new outlook is through discussion with others about the benefits to be derived from it. It's important not to become dogmatic about your new knowledge (for example, 'You *have* to be self-accepting, self-esteem doesn't work'), develop a holier-than-thou attitude (for example, 'My new way of seeing things in life really emphasises the myopia of others') or expect to have all the answers when others find your views unpersuasive or full of flaws (reflecting on their comments can help you to build stronger arguments). Also, when others (for example, family members or friends) seek your advice, ensure that you really are practising what you preach otherwise your inconsistencies will become readily apparent (for example, 'Hey, Mr Hypocrite, why are you getting so angry because I disagree with you? I thought you advocated tolerance of different viewpoints'). Finally, teaching your children how to be resilient in facing life's challenges can be one of your most enduring legacies to them.

Conclusion

We're often told by people that they felt inspired after reading a particular self-help book. Unfortunately, inspiration is not always followed by action or, if it is, the action is not usually sustained (for example, 'It's very stimulating reading about getting more out of yourself and your life but when it comes to actually doing it, that's another story altogether, isn't it?'). Don't let this happen to you. If this book or any part of it has interested you or even seized your imagination, then commit yourself to and persist with an action plan to achieve your desired goals of increased personal effectiveness in your chosen area or areas. One final thought: you can waste so much time in your life by not going after what you really want that you might believe, at odd moments, that you actually have several lives available to you instead of only one. So don't waste any more time – act now!

References

Adair, J. (1988) *Effective Time Management*. London: Pan books.

Arnold, J., Cooper, C. L. and Robertson, I. T. (1995) *Work Psychology: Understanding Human Behaviour in the Workplace*, 2nd edn. London: Pitman Publishing.

Atkinson, J. M. (1994) *Coping with Stress at Work*. London: Thorsons.

Baggini, J. and Macaro, A. (2012) *The Shrink and the Sage*. London: Icon Books.

Baumeister, R. F. and Tierney, J. (2012) *Willpower: Rediscovering Our Greatest Strength*. London: Allen Lane.

Beck, A. T. (1976) *Cognitive Therapy and the Emotional Disorders*. New York: International Universities Press.

Beck, A. T., Rush, A. J., Shaw, B. F. and Emery, G. (1979) *Cognitive Therapy of Depression*. New York: Guilford.

Beck, A. T., Wright, F. D., Newman, C. F. and Liese, B. S. (1993) *Cognitive Therapy of Substance Abuse*. New York: Guilford.

Beck, J. S. (2011) *Cognitive Behavior Therapy: Basics and Beyond*, 2nd edn. New York: Guilford.

Berlin, I. (1998) 'Two concepts of liberty', in H. Hardy and R. Hausheer, eds., *The Proper Study of Mankind: An Anthology of Essays by Isaiah Berlin*. London: Pimlico.

Bernard, M. E. (1993) 'Are your emotions and behaviors helping you or hurting you?', in M. E. Bernard and J. L. Wolfe, eds., *The RET Resource Book for Practitioners*. New York: The Albert Ellis Institute for Rational Emotive Behavior Therapy.

Bishay, N. R., Tarrier, N., Dolan, M., Beckett, R. and Harwood, S. (1996) 'Morbid jealousy: a cognitive outlook', *Journal of Cognitive Psychotherapy*, 10(1): 9–22.

Buckley, A. and Buckley, C. (2006) *A Guide to Coaching and Mental Health*. Hove: Routledge.

Burkeman, O. (2012) *The Antidote: Happiness for People Who Can't Stand Positive Thinking*. London: Canongate Books.

Burns, D. D. (1980) 'The perfectionist's script for self-defeat', *Psychology Today*, November: 34–57.

Burns, D. D. (1981) *Feeling Good: The New Mood Therapy*. New York: Signet.

Burns, D. D. (1989) *The Feeling Good Handbook*. New York: William Morrow.

Butler, G. and McManus, F. (2000) *Psychology: A Very Short Introduction*, reissued. Oxford: Oxford University Press.

Butler, G. and Hope, T. (2007) *Manage Your Mind: The Mental Fitness Guide*, 2nd edn. Oxford: Oxford University Press.

Cain, S. (2012) *Quiet: The Power of Introverts in a World That Can't Stop Talking*. London: Viking.

Chesney, M. A. and Rosenman, R. H. (1985) *Anger and Hostility in Cardiovascular and Behavioral Disorders*. Washington, DC: Hemisphere.

Clark, D. A. and Beck, A. T. (2012) *The Anxiety and Worry Workbook: The Cognitive Behavioral Solution*. New York: Guilford.

Cormier, W. H. and Cormier, L. S. (1985) *Interviewing Strategies for Helpers: Fundamental Skills and Cognitive Behavioral Interventions*, 2nd edn. Monterey, CA: Brooks/Cole.

Covey, S. R. (1989) *The 7 Habits of Highly Effective People*. New York: Simon & Schuster.

Crews, F. (2006) *Follies of the Wise: Dissenting Essays*. Emeryville, CA: Shoemaker & Hoard.

Davis, M., Eshelman, E. R. and McKay, M. (1995) *The Relaxation and Stress Reduction Workbook*, 4th edn. Oakland, CA: New Harbinger Publications.

DiGiuseppe, R. (1995) 'Developing the therapeutic alliance with angry clients', in H. Kassinove, ed., *Anger Disorders: Definition, Diagnosis, and Treatment*. Bristol, PA: Taylor & Francis.

DiMattia, D. and IJzermans, T. (2011) *CBT in Action: Applications in the Workplace*, 2nd edn. Mentone, Australia: CBT Australia.

Dobbin, R. (2008) (trans. and ed.) *Epictetus: Discourses and Selected Writings*. London: Penguin.

Dryden, W. (2000) *Overcoming Procrastination*. London: Sheldon.

Dryden, W. (2009) *Self-Discipline: How to Get It and How to Keep It*. London: Sheldon.

Dryden, W. and Gordon, J. (1993) *Beating the Comfort Trap*. London: Sheldon.

Dryden, W. and Gordon, J. (1994) *How to Cope When the Going Gets Tough*. London: Sheldon.

Dryden, W. and Matweychuk, W. (2000) *Overcoming Your Addictions*. London: Sheldon.

Edelman, S. (2006) *Change Your Thinking*. London: Vermilion.

Ehrenreich, B. (2009) *Smile or Die: How Positive Thinking Fooled America and the World*. London: Granta.

Ellis, A. (1979) *RET and Assertiveness Training*, audiocassette. New York: Albert Ellis Institute for Rational Emotive Behavior Therapy.

Ellis, A. (1994) *Reason and Emotion in Psychotherapy*, revised and updated. New York: Birch Lane Press.

Ellis, A. (1996) 'The treatment of morbid jealousy: a rational emotive behavior therapy approach', *Journal of Cognitive Psychotherapy*, 10(1): 23–33.

Ellis, A. (2002) *Overcoming Resistance: a Rational Emotive Behavior Therapy Integrated Approach*, 2nd edn. New York: Springer.

Ellis, A. and Knaus, W. J. (1977) *Overcoming Procrastination*. New York: Albert Ellis Institute for Rational Emotive Behavior Therapy.

Ellis, A., McInerney, J. F., DiGiuseppe, R. and Yeager, R. J. (1988) *Rational-Emotive Therapy with Alcoholics and Substance Abusers*. New York: Pergamon.

Flach, F. (2004) *Resilience: Discovering a New Strength at Times of Stress*, 2nd edn. New York: Hatherleigh Press.

Fontana, D. (1989) *Managing Stress*. London: BPS and Routledge.

Forward, S. (1997) *Emotional Blackmail*. London: Bantam Books.

Frankl, V. E. (1985) *Man's Search for Meaning*. New York: Washington Square Press. (Originally published in German in 1946.)

Furnham, A. (1996) *The Myths of Management*. London: Whurr.

Furnham, A. (2012) 'Why a dose of confidence is key to showing humility', *The Sunday Times*, 1st July.

Gilbert, P. (1989) *Human Nature and Suffering*. Hove: Lawrence Erlbaum Associates.

Gilbert, P. (1997) *Overcoming Depression*. London: Robinson.

Gilbert, P. (1998) 'Shame and humiliation in the treatment of complex cases', in N. Tarrier, A. Wells and G. Haddock, eds., *Treating Complex Cases: The Cognitive Behavioural Therapy Approach*. Chichester: John Wiley.

Gilbert, P. (2000) *Counselling for Depression*, 2nd edn. London: Sage.

Grayling, A. C. (2002) *The Meaning of Things: Applying Philosophy to Life*. London: Phoenix.

Grayling, A. C. (2009) *Ideas That Matter: A Personal Guide for the 21st Century*. London: Weidenfeld & Nicolson.

Grayling, A. C. (2010) *Thinking of Answers: Questions in the Philosophy of Everyday Life*. London: Bloomsbury.

Grieger, R. M. (1991) 'Keys to effective RET', in M. E. Bernard (ed.), *Using Rational-Emotive Therapy Effectively: A Practitioner's Guide*. New York: Plenum.

Grieger, R. and Boyd, J. (1980) *Rational-Emotive Therapy: A Skills-Based Approach*. New York: Van Nostrand Reinhold.

Grotberg, E. H. (2001) *Tapping Your Inner Strength: How to Find the Resilience to Deal with Anything*. New Delhi, India: New Age Books.

Haidt, J. (2006) *The Happiness Hypothesis: Putting Ancient Wisdom and Philosophy to the Test of Modern Science*. London: Arrow.

Hauck, P. (1974) *Depression*. London: Sheldon.

Hauck, P. (1980) *Calm Down*. London: Sheldon.

Hauck, P. (1981a) *Why Be Afraid?* London: Sheldon.

Hauck, P. (1981b) *How to Stand Up for Yourself.* London: Sheldon.

Hauck, P. (1982a) *Jealousy.* London: Sheldon.

Hauck, P. (1982b) *How to Do What You Want to Do.* London: Sheldon.

Hauck, P. (1988) *How to Be Your Own Best Friend.* London: Sheldon.

Hauck, P. (1991a) 'RET and the assertive process', in M. E. Bernard, ed., *Using Rational-Emotive Therapy Effectively: A Practitioner's Guide.* New York: Plenum.

Hauck, P. (1991b) *Hold Your Head Up High.* London: Sheldon.

Hitchens, C. (1995) *The Missionary Position: Mother Teresa in Theory and Practice.* London: Verso.

Hitchens, C. (2012) *Mortality.* London: Atlantic.

Horney, K. (1950) *Neurosis and Human Growth.* New York: Norton.

Irvine, W. B. (2009) *A Guide to the Good Life: The Ancient Art of Stoic Joy.* New York: Oxford University Press.

Jakubowski, P. and Lange, A. J. (1978) *The Assertive Option.* Champaign, IL: Research Press.

Jones, K. (1998) *Time Management: The Essential Guide to Thinking and Working Smarter.* London: Marshall Publishing.

Keller, H. (1903/2007) *The Story of My Life.* Teddington: Echo Library.

Kleinke, C. L. (1991) *Coping with Life Challenges.* Pacific Grove, CA: Brooks/Cole.

Knaus, W. (1998) *Do It Now!*, 2nd edn. New York: Wiley.

Knaus, W. (2010) *End Procrastination Now! Get it Done With a Proven Psychological Approach.* New York: McGraw-Hill.

Lange, A. J. and Jakubowski, P. (1976) *Responsible Assertive Behavior: Cognitive/Behavioral Procedures for Trainers.* Champaign, IL: Research Press.

Lazarus, A. A. (1977) 'Towards an egoless state of being', in A. Ellis and R. Grieger, eds., *Handbook of Rational-Emotive Therapy.* New York: Springer.

Lazarus, R. S. (1999) *Stress and Emotion.* London: Free Association Books.

Lazarus, R. S. and Folkman, S. (1984) *Stress, Appraisal and Coping.* New York: Springer.

Leahy, R. L. (1996) *Cognitive Therapy: Basic Principles and Applications.* Northvale, NJ: Jason Aronson Inc.

Leahy, R. L. (1999) 'Strategic self-limitation', *Journal of Cognitive Psychotherapy*, 13(4): 275–293.

Leahy, R. L. (2006) *The Worry Cure.* London: Piatkus Books.

Leahy, R. L. (2010) *Beat the Blues Before They Beat You: How to Overcome Depression.* New York: Hay House.

Mann, S. (1998) *Psychology Goes to Work.* Oxford: Purple House.

Masten, A. S. and O' Dougherty Wright, M. (2010) 'Resilience over the lifespan: developmental perspectives on resistance, recovery, and transformation', in J. W. Reich, A. J. Zautra and J. S. Hall, eds, *Handbook of Adult Resilience.* New York: Guilford.

McKay, M., Davis, M. and Fanning, P. (2011) *Thoughts and Feelings: Taking Control of Your Moods and Your Life*, 4th edn. Oakland, CA: New Harbinger Publications.

Meichenbaum, D. (2012) *Roadmap to Resilience: A Guide for Military, Trauma Victims and Their Families*. Clearwater, FL: Institute Press.

Mooney, K. A. and Padesky, C. A. (2000) 'Applying client creativity to recurrent problems: constructing possibilities and tolerating doubt', *Journal of Cognitive Psychotherapy*, 14(2): 149–161.

Moran, Lord (Charles Wilson) (1945/2007) *The Anatomy of Courage*. London: Robinson.

Neenan, M. (2009) *Developing Resilience: A Cognitive-Behavioural Approach*. Hove: Routledge.

Neenan, M. and Palmer, S. (2012) *Cognitive Behavioural Coaching in Practice: An Evidence Based Approach*. Hove: Routledge.

Newman, C. F. (2000) 'Hypotheticals in cognitive psychotherapy: creative questions, novel answers, and therapeutic change', *Journal of Cognitive Psychotherapy*, 14(2): 135–147.

Nezu, A. M., Nezu, C. M. and D'Zurilla, T. J. (2007) *Solving Life's Problems: A 5-Step Guide to Enhanced Well-Being*. New York: Springer.

NICE(2005) *Clinical Guidelines for Treating Mental Health Problems*. London: National Institute for Health and Clinical Excellence.

Northedge, A. (1990) *The Good Study Guide*. Milton Keynes: Open University.

O'Connell Higgins, G. (1994) *Resilient Adults: Overcoming a Cruel Past*. San Francisco, CA: Jossey-Bass.

Padesky, C. A. (1993) 'Schema as self-prejudice', *International Cognitive Therapy Newsletter*, 5/6:16–17.

Padesky, C. A. and Greenberger, D. (1995) *Clinician's Guide to Mind over Mood*. New York: Guilford.

Palmer, S. and Dryden, W. (1995) *Counselling for Stress Problems*. London: Sage.

Persaud, R. (2005) *The Motivated Mind*. London: Bantam.

Pinker, S. (2011) *The Better Angels of Our Nature*. London: Allen Lane.

Quick, J. C., Wright, T. A., Adkins, J. A., Nelson, D. L. and Quick, J. D. (2013) *Preventive Stress Management in Organizations*, 2nd edn. Washington, DC: American Psychological Association.

Reivich, K. and Shatté, A. (2002) *The Resilience Factor: 7 Keys to Finding Your Inner Strength and Overcoming Life's Hurdles*. New York: Broadway Books.

Robb, H. B. (1992) 'Why you don't have a "perfect right" to anything', *Journal of Rational-Emotive & Cognitive-Behavior Therapy*, 10(4): 259–270.

Robertson, D. (2010) *The Philosophy of Cognitive-Behavioural Therapy (CBT): Stoic Philosophy as Rational and Cognitive Psychotherapy*. London: Karnac.

Robertson, D. (2012) *Build Your Resilience: How to Survive and Thrive in Any Situation*. London: Hodder Education.

Sapadin, L. and Maguire, J. (1996) *It's About Time!* New York: Penguin.

Schulz, K. (2010) *Being Wrong: Adventures in the Margin of Error*. London: Portobello Books.

Sheldon, B. (1995) *Cognitive-Behavioural Therapy: Research, Practice and Philosophy*. London: Routledge.

Sherman, N. (2005) *Stoic Warriors: The Ancient Philosophy Behind the Military Mind*. New York: Oxford University Press.

Sichel, J. (1993) 'Values clarification', in M. E. Bernard and J. L. Wolfe, eds., *The RET Resource Book for Practitioners*. New York: Albert Ellis Institute for Rational Emotive Behavior Therapy.

Southwick, S. M. and Charney, D. S. (2012) *Resilience: The Science of Mastering Life's Greatest Challenges*. New York: Cambridge University Press.

Steinberg, P. (2001) *Speak You Also: A Survivor's Reckoning*. London: Allen Lane.

Stockdale, J. B. (1993) *Courage Under Fire: Testing Epictetus's Doctrines in a Laboratory of Human Behavior* (Hoover Essays). Stanford, CA: Hoover Institution Press.

Tavris, C. (2011*) Psychobabble and Biobunk: Using Psychological Science to Think Critically About Popular Psychology*, 3rd edn. London: Prentice Hall.

Trower, P., Jones, J., Dryden, W. and Casey, A. (2011) *Cognitive-Behavioural Counselling in Action*, 2nd edn. London: SAGE.

Walen, S. R., DiGiuseppe, R. and Dryden, W. (1992) *A Practitioner's Guide to Rational-Emotive Therapy*, 2nd edn. New York: Oxford University Press.

Wessler, R. A. and Wessler, R. L. (1980) *The Principles and Practice of Rational–Emotive Therapy*. San Francisco, CA: Jossey-Bass.

Williams, M. and Penman, D. (2011) *Mindfulness: A Practical Guide to Finding Peace in a Frantic World*. London: Piatkus.

Wiseman, R. (2009) *59 Seconds: Think a Little, Change a Lot*. London: Macmillan.

Index